# AMERICA'S
# LOST
## OPPORTUNITY

Sept. 20, 2014

Mike,

Hope you enjoy reading this book. Thanks for your support!

Deborah K. Smith

# AMERICA'S
# LOST
## OPPORTUNITY

## STOLEN VICTORIES 2012

### (A CITIZEN'S ACCOUNT)

## DEBORAH K. SMARTH

Rev. date: 08/16/2013

**To order additional copies of this book, contact:**
Xlibris LLC
1-888-795-4274
www.Xlibris.com
Orders@Xlibris.com
135753

# CONTENTS

Introduction...........................................................................................7

Chapter 1:  Winning the Delegates ..........................................................23
Chapter 2:  On to Tampa: The Republican National Convention ........47
Chapter 3:  Media Blackout: Marginalization of a Presidential
            Candidate of Great Integrity, Vision, and a
            Champion of Liberty.............................................................72
Chapter 4:  Post-Tampa Convention, Election Day, and Its Aftermath .....90
Chapter 5:  Ron Paul Support Grows Abroad.....................................116
Chapter 6:  Conclusion .........................................................................122

The Founding Principles of Government as Stated
    in the Declaration of Independence...............................................134

Quotations that Matter ......................................................................135

Index...................................................................................................141

Many photos used in this book are the courtesy of
Gage Skidmore, photographer.

# INTRODUCTION

AS A CITIZEN who watched the 2011-2012 presidential campaign unfold, I curiously researched and read as much as I could possibly obtain via the Internet. I soon realized that the election process and the reporting by the mainstream media did not seem transparent enough. There was a large gap between what I was learning via alternate sources and what was being reported on by the corporate media. The American people and specifically the voting electorate were not getting the necessary information to make truly informed decisions about whom they should consider casting their vote in the November 2012 presidential election.

In December 2011 and through 2012, I viewed as many presidential candidates' speeches in the lead-up to the early primaries and caucuses for the Republican nomination. A large field of candidates existed, indeed, but eventually, the race narrowed to only two Republican candidates: former Republican governor Mitt Romney of Massachusetts and longtime, twelve-term Republican congressman Ron Paul from Texas. In his earlier years, Paul had served as a veteran acting as a medical flight surgeon in the air force and the Air National Guard during the Vietnam War. As a medical doctor, obstetrician, he delivered over four thousand babies. He was not only a true fiscal Conservative, but a die-hard Libertarian; and his commitment to less taxation, less government spending, a smaller government, the U.S. Constitution, and a rational foreign policy and strong defense was continually documented by his voting record in the U.S. Congress. Many referred to him as Dr. No.

Paul never voted to raise taxes, never voted for an unbalanced budget, never voted to raise congressional pay, never took a government-paid junket, never voted to increase the power of the executive branch, voted against regulating the Internet, and never participated in the lucrative congressional pension program. He was continually named the Taxpayers' Best Friend in Congress. Lobbyists at the Capitol didn't even bother to meet with the congressman since he was not beholden to any special interests.

In fact, as he said when questioned during one of the 2012 GOP presidential debates, he would bring a "bushel of common sense" to the workings of Washington, D.C., as president. He is also the congressman that returned almost $1.5 million in unused congressional office funds to the United States Treasury during his tenure as a member of Congress. He pledged, if elected to the presidency, to only take a $39,300 annual salary to align with the median salary of the American worker. The president of the United States draws a $400,000 salary. He is one of those rare elected officials who led by example.

Having been affiliated with both political parties in my earlier years, I became an Independent voter following the debacle of the Bush administration. Bush described himself as a "compassionate" Conservative. During the first administration and subsequent four-year term, the mantra of "Conservative"—being fiscally prudent—lapsed. The national deficit and debt were increasing under his presidential administration as it has even further increased under the Obama administration. During the Obama administration, the national debt increased to $16.687 trillion from $10.626 trillion when Obama took office. Under Bush, the debt increased by $4.9 trillion.[1] But what bothered me the most focused on the war hawk position promoted by the Neoconservatives who seemed to have hijacked the Republican Party and, more importantly, turned upside-down the very concepts of a Jeffersonian "republic" on which our U.S. Constitution is based.

Jefferson, as a Founding Father, had promoted that foreign policy should be based on commerce relationships to essentially result in peaceful relations to avoid war. Jefferson said, "Peace and friendship with all mankind is our wisest policy, and I wish we may be permitted to pursue it." He was further quoted as saying, "Unlike those nations whose rulers use their country's resources to seek conquests, to carry on warring contests with one another, and consequently plunge their people into

---

[1]   Sandy Fitzgerald, "National debt up more than $6 trillion under Obama," Newsmax, http://www.newsmax.com, March 2, 2013.

DEBORAH K. SMARTH

debt and devastation, free societies are organized for the happiness and prosperity of their people, and this is best pursued in a state of peace."

The entrance of America into the Iraq War under false pretenses and rationale, later documented by the fact that no weapons of mass destruction were found, further added to my question-raising in the political realm. The fact that so many congressional members up on Capitol Hill had let this war occur and then subsequently allowed us to enter and create a troop surge into Afghanistan bothered me even further like so many other Americans. One congressman, Ron Paul, voted against such military actions.

More than 6,600 men and women in our armed services who served in the Iraq and Afghanistan conflicts were killed,[2] notwithstanding thousands and thousands more suffering from post-traumatic stress syndrome and disabled veterans who lost their limbs or who were severely mentally disabled. For the first time in history, the military is experiencing larger suicide rates by its Iraq and Afghanistan veterans than in past wars. Thousands upon thousands of innocent men, women, and children in Iraq and Afghanistan became victims of war. Some studies report that as of January 2013, in Iraq alone, up to 121,736 Iraqi civilian deaths occurred;[3] and since the United Nations started reporting statistics in 2007 through 2012, an additional 13,009 Afghan civilian deaths were reported.[4] However, the Lancet study "found in 2006 that almost 650,000 Iraqis, both civilians and fighters, had died from the war up until that point."[5] Other credible research indicates that "more than 1 million Iraqis were killed, with 4.5 million displaced."[6] Not to mention the trillions of taxpayers' dollars that the American military industrial complex has spent at a time when America itself is technically bankrupt. I simply thought, *Is this the America we are becoming?* The Iraq War has cost $1.7 trillion;

---

2    http://www.icasualties.org (accessed March 3, 2013).

3    http://www.Iraqbodycount.org/ (accessed March 3, 2013).

4    Susan Chesser, "Afghanistan Casualties: Military forces and civilians," Congressional Research Service, http://www.fas.org/sgp/crs/natsec/R41084. pdf, December 6, 2012, 3.

5    John Glaser, "Iraq war could cost $6 trillion," http://news.antiwar.com, March 14, 2013.

6    Ibid.

however, "the cost could grow to more than $6 trillion over the next four decades when interest payments are included."[7]

The one leader in Congress, also a Republican presidential candidate, who advocated for the complete embracing of the U.S. Constitution and its principles and who fully promoted in his presidential campaign an end to the unnecessary, pre-emptive wars overseas, was Dr. Ron Paul, congressman from Texas. Despite the political and media establishment's unfair, limited, and negative coverage, he continued throughout his presidential campaign to remind people of his no votes on the war issue. His positions were motivated by the Jeffersonian concepts that we should be engaging with countries and dialoguing with countries to avoid war, that war should always be a last resort. Yet, as Michael Scheuer, former CIA intelligence officer and supporter of Ron Paul's presidential candidacy, said, "Paul's call for staying out of other people's wars unless genuine U.S. national interests are at stake is deemed radical, immoral, even, anti-American. Amazing." That was the kind of perception and image the media and establishment tried to portray of Republican presidential candidate Ron Paul.

What struck me most while I watched and listened to vignettes (via the Internet) of Republican presidential candidate Ron Paul's speeches across the nation was his resounding commitment to a sound economic policy and rational foreign policy. He was the one candidate who actually had a specific plan to eliminate the debt and deficit in America. His platform called for the abolishment of five federal agencies and the reduction in U.S. Defense spending in areas that were no longer needed, including military bases that were in countries which are strong allies, like Germany, Japan, etc.

In fact, he not only outlined the mission and vision for the country but, unlike most politicians, also provided a litany of specific items to achieve the incremental reduction of the country's sixteen-trillion-plus national debt. In his first year as president, his plan to "Restore America Now" called for slashing $1 trillion in spending and would have balanced the budget by the third year of his presidency. Included in that platform, he was freely speaking about the Federal Reserve system and the creation of money out of thin air, whereby the "big institutions" regularly receive monies at zero-interest or below-market rates from the Federal Reserve, while the regular working people and middle class pay higher interest

---

[7]   Ibid.

rates on borrowed money. All one needs to do as a consumer is look at the usurious rates of interest that the large credit card companies charge on the purchase of products and services. Look at the bailout of major financial institutions through TARP with our tax dollars when individuals and small businesses do not receive that same treatment!

But more importantly, Dr. Paul was making speeches at college campuses across the nation where thousands of students and individuals residing in campus areas and other geographic locations would listen intently and then provide resounding approval through applause that was thunderous. I decided one day to travel to Philadelphia for one of his rallies on April 22, 2012, and in the pouring rain, I listened to his speech along with four-thousand-plus Americans who traveled great distances to this metropolitan center to hear his views and vision. It was held on the south side of Independence Mall, a perfect location for a constitutionalist. I thought, *Oh, how other elected officials could only wish they had such a following!* It was terrific to see an enthusiastic crowd of listeners in all age groups, but especially our youth. Republican state senator Michael Doherty (R-New Jersey) greeted Paul on stage with encouraging words, and former CIA Bin Laden unit chief Michael Scheuer also made a speech before Paul greeted this large crowd which waited in enthusiastic anticipation of Dr. Paul's address. The crowd here, just as those crowds at other rallies around the nation (seen via the Internet), would chant, "President Paul" and "End the Fed." The fact that Paul was able to attract such large crowds with such a committed following was always quite endearing and impressive to me. At the University of California-Berkeley, 8,500-plus attendees applauded Paul's liberty message, and crowds in the thousands would normally show up at campus events throughout the country to see and listen to his robust, knowledge-packed speeches.

But unfortunately, other than sometimes local network affiliates, the national media rarely broadcast the thousands and thousands that showed up for these types of events across the nation. Thus, the surge in Dr. Paul's strong grassroots support did not get further bolstered by media coverage despite his very strong showings in the early and subsequent primaries and caucuses. He received no bumps as other GOP candidates would get from the national media coverage provided to them. In fact, even after strong electoral showings in such contests, the media seemed to talk or report about it in a dismissive way. After following this campaign day after day through the Tampa national convention, it became apparent that the mainstream media (MSM) tried forcefully to label and describe his candidacy as "unelectable." Unelectable by whom? I asked. My reaction as well as that of millions of others who followed and supported his candidacy was—unlike all other GOP early contenders and the Democratic incumbent president—Paul was the only statesman and true patriot who was challenging the pre-ordained positions of both national parties and their elite interests for years. More importantly, his voting record in Congress matched those ideals and beliefs he promoted during his presidential campaign, something that the other candidates couldn't even begin to parallel with the flip-flopping that occurs regularly in the political process.

Paul challenged them on sound money, advocating for a transparent central banking system and introducing his "Audit the Fed" bill, HR 459; he challenged them on pre-emptive war, promoting it as a last resort and made a pledge to bring home the troops day 1 of a Paul administration. He challenged them on Mideast policy, strongly emphasizing that all foreign aid should go away. In addition, he acknowledged strongly that our Mideast policies have blowback from the Arab-Muslim world and make us less safe. He advocated greater dialogue to forcefully engage and solve problems rather than executing aggressive, militaristic policies that promote more blowback, hatred, and violent acts against America. Finally, Dr. Paul challenged his opponents and the political establishment by saying that spending cuts had to be more than make-believe cuts on automatic program-spending increases that occur each year in the congressional budgetary process. He further pointed out that the unending spending of a federal government, aided and abetted by a Federal Reserve System, which prints monies without currency backup, thereby devaluing the dollar over time, must stop. He acknowledged that America is bankrupt, and thus our national defense and domestic policies must be adjusted accordingly. His proposed policies did just that!

Despite his good, solid showings in the initial 2012 GOP primaries and caucuses, the media and political establishment undercut his candidacy of intellectual ideas that were pragmatic for these times. Despite the fact that he was a Republican presidential candidate who participated in the debates that were held as well as the fact that he had served in the U.S. Congress for more than two decades as a Republican, the media talking heads would make it appear that he was a third-party candidate, pressing his Libertarian positions when they referenced him occasionally. But these primaries and caucuses—as is often the case—were simply "beauty contests." The path to the Republican nomination would be based on the votes of delegates to the Republican state conventions. The rules of the national committee did in fact provide that the delegate votes at these state conventions would contribute to the national delegates to the GOP national convention in Tampa.

All Americans should shudder at the occurrences in these state GOP conventions across the country. Along the way to the state GOP conventions, there would be precinct, county, and district gatherings. The delegates there would go on to the state conventions. Presidential candidate Ron Paul won the majority of delegates in as many as eight-state Republican conventions through sheer Republican grassroots participation and support. They were regular people, many of them youth, who, because of their solid support for Dr. Paul's platform, attended these state GOP conventions. Many of the Republican supporters of Dr. Paul who gave of their time to participate as delegates at these many state GOP conventions were not part of the regular party committees and organizations. Their intent was to try and convince other party insiders that Dr. Paul had the right ideas for these most difficult times and that indeed these ideas were not cookie cutter at all but represented something new and different. Paul's ideas were prudent and needed more than ever at this time in history. Despite their self-education on the rules of the respective state conventions, including Robert's Rules of Order, the processes and practices at these conventions proved unfair and downright unethical sometimes. There is plenty of evidence about these unseemly occurrences and unfair treatment by the GOP establishment in YouTube and other Internet videos taken at these conventions as well as many state newspaper accounts. These various examples will be discussed in this book.

Then there is the outright fraud that existed during the pre-Tampa convention rules adoption and the attempts that were made by state and national party leaders to de-credential the Ron Paul delegates who legitimately won support at these individual state GOP conventions leading up to Tampa. Did you know that in Massachusetts, the state from which Mitt Romney was governor, presidential candidate Ron Paul won the majority of delegates at the GOP statewide caucus? Yes, there was reference to it in the *Boston Globe* when the GOP regulars and the party apparatus tried tirelessly to reverse the numbers that Ron Paul's grassroots army won fairly and squarely. Similar underhanded attempts occurred at other state conventions in Arizona, Colorado, Louisiana, Maine, Missouri, Nevada, Oklahoma, Oregon, and other places too.

GOP national party rules provided that if a presidential candidate won a plurality of delegates in five or more states, that candidate's name could be placed in nomination and that candidate would be entitled to address the national Republican convention. While all the other GOP presidential candidates, like Governor Rick Perry (Texas), Congresswoman Michele Bachmann (Minnesota), entrepreneur Herman Cain, former governor Jon Huntsman (Utah), former governor Tim Pawlenty (Minnesota), former speaker Newt Gingrich (Georgia), and former senator Rick Santorum (Pennsylvania), could not raise enough campaign funds or grassroots delegates to succeed in going to Tampa, Republican presidential candidate Ron Paul did. His grassroots support not only provided an army of delegates won at state GOP conventions, but also provided millions and millions of dollars in campaign contributions from the beginning to end through his money bomb appeals. Unlike all the other GOP contenders, including Mitt Romney, Paul's monetary support came from the grassroots, including the military men and women, not from the institutional and corporate interests that ruled the day. Big-time financier and billionaire casino magnate Sheldon Adelson from Nevada reportedly kept Newt Gingrich's initial campaign efforts afloat and then subsequently pumped, along with his family, "well over the $100 million he had vowed to spend to help" the Romney-Republican Party's efforts to attain a November election victory.[8]

As the national GOP convention policy and rules committees met in Tampa prior to the official commencement of the GOP national convention, activities occurred to further thwart any surprises that could raise the consciousness of the American people, or for that matter, the regular rank-and-file party members, who served as delegates at the national convention. In order to prevent up to five hundred delegates that were won by Dr. Paul throughout the state conventions process, the individual state Republican Party apparatus in collaboration with the Republican National Committee (RNC) attempted to and did in fact de-credential Paul delegates in certain states. Evidently, these actions were undertaken to change the outcomes relating to the five states' plurality of delegates requirement for placing a name in nomination for president. It became apparent that the Republican leaders' attempts to de-credential

---

8   Nicholas Confessore and Derek Willis, "2012 Election ended with deluge of donations and spending," New York Times, http://thecaucusblogs.nytimes.com, December 7, 2012.

Paul delegates were related to quelling a come-from-behind win like President Warren Harding. One thing the political establishment did not want was the possibility of having presidential candidate Ron Paul addressing the national convention on domestic, economic, and foreign policy issues of importance, promoting certain Libertarian views within the Republican Party. They succeeded in doing so.

The governor of Maine, Governor Paul LePage, a Republican who supported Mitt Romney, actually boycotted the national convention because of the de-credentialing of Ron Paul delegates who won the Maine GOP state convention. The RNC prevented the potential defections of regular party members seated at the national convention as delegates to Ron Paul's camp by changing the rules to disallow Paul's name from going into nomination and making a speech to a thirty-five-million-plus audience who would be viewing this national convention. Could defections have occurred? One observation is for sure. A Ron Paul speech would have presented an issues platform colored by sheer rationality and common sense and in sharp contradistinction to the strongly vested and elite interests to pursue the same Neoconservative views of war hawk and the persistence of more government spending by the unending printing of money out of thin air by the Federal Reserve.

There were all-out efforts by the national Republican Party and Romney campaign to completely change the rules of the party to prevent another grassroots presidential delegate campaign from ever arising again, thereby preventing regular folks and voters who want to civically engage to catalyze a presidential candidate from the grassroots. By changing the national party rules on delegate selection at state GOP conventions, it appears that the party was aiming to ensure that no future scenarios of the kind witnessed during the Ron Paul state convention delegate majorities can ever occur again.

Despite the frantic actions of a national party bent on a Mitt Romney candidacy, Paul's campaign continued until the end in Tampa. But Paul's sound ideas and the intellectual revolution he has propelled continue presently and into the future. While the Paul delegates were successful in getting the national GOP Policy Committee to include several positions held by Dr. Paul, it was evident in the Romney campaign that presidential candidate Mitt Romney did not advocate strongly or reference many of these adopted party planks. In fact, while his first debate showed an upward surge for his candidacy against incumbent President Obama, the second debate on foreign policy showed there was little difference between

Obama and Romney, with Romney mostly agreeing with Obama's positions, including the use of unmanned drones. In January 2013, the United Nations launched an investigation into the legality of the U.S. drone program, which has until recently remained highly secretive and unexamined.

While candidates from both major parties elected to Congress and other governing bodies pretend to have major differences on government spending, taxation, war, and economic policies, the fact is they are becoming more and more alike. That's why no real change ever occurs in national politics and policies. The only presidential candidate in 2012 who presented a real difference in ideas and solutions was Congressman and Dr. Ron Paul from Texas. But the political establishment and corporate media prevented many people from knowing him or his true positions. His positions and outreach was largely done through the Internet, blogs, and through limited but targeted campaign resources. Certain Pew research studies document that Paul received way less coverage than all other GOP presidential candidates.

Ron Paul was truthful and courageous, taking on the most powerful interests by challenging the Federal Reserve System, promoting a trillion-dollar spending cut in his first year in office, ending both the Iraq and Afghanistan involvements immediately and exemplifying and defining liberty in its truest form. His revolution focuses on the role of government as purported and expounded by the Founding Fathers of our great nation. He even advocated for the abolishment of the income tax and potential replacement with a national consumption tax which would be fairer since taxpayers in different income categories would pay their fair share on the value of their goods purchased. Wouldn't this be a real check on federal government spending?

Paul continually, throughout the campaign and in the now-alive Liberty movement he founded, said that Americans should keep the fruits of their own labor, thereby diminishing the welfare state and promoting maximum levels of liberty. Paul said, "One thing is clear: The Founding Fathers never intended a nation where citizens would pay nearly half of everything they earn to the government."

And how true is this now when the federal government and other levels of government take 50 percent or more of Americans' hard-earned dollars? "This simple idea, that government should stay out of the looting business and leave people to their own pursuits, has had great moral appeal throughout U.S. history," says Paul.[9] He further references the great political and economic writers of all time, Frederic Bastiat, concerning legal plunder on the part of government, which is diminishing economic freedom by taking away more from people's rights to their life and property.

In addition, he was the only national candidate who wanted to talk about how America's military structure and defense system is being used to engage in unnecessary wars that are undeclared and how aggressive foreign engagements drain monies from the citizens of this nation. Did you know that the major media never aired or broadcast a demonstration of hundreds of military veterans returning from the Iraq and Afghanistan wars who marched to the White House? They chanted "President Paul" because they understood and fully supported the kind of military and foreign policy that Paul embraced. They did an about-face, turning their backs away from the White House, in opposition to the Obama administration's militaristic policies. In fact, it was reported that veterans contributed the most to Paul's presidential campaign out of all the eight GOP candidates seeking the presidential nomination, including President Barack Obama!

Paul was also the only candidate talking about the increase in unmanned drone strikes under the Obama administration, where innocent civilians are being killed as a result. Along with several other congressional members, Paul joined in sending a letter to the president, asking for clarification of criteria for the lethal use of drones overseas and warned against the potentially more harmful effects by creating more enemies than it eliminates. A recently released September 25, 2012, report from the Stanford and New York University law schools found that initial and follow-up drone strikes have led to the deaths of rescuers and medical professionals as well as widespread post-traumatic stress disorder and "an overall breakdown of functional society" in certain locations in Pakistan. The Bureau of Investigative Journalism reported that since June 2004 through mid-September 2012, existing data indicates that U.S. drones have killed up to 3,325 people in Pakistan, including up to 881 innocent civilians and 176 children.[10] The study's interviewees said, "They

---

[9] Ron Paul, *The Revolution: A Manifesto* (New York/Boston: Grand Central Publishing), 2008, p. 70-71.

[10] "Executive summary and recommendations," http://www.livingunderdrones. org, September 2012.

didn't know what America was before drones. Now, what they know of America is drones, death and terror."[11] In addition to speaking out about drones, Ron Paul was the only presidential candidate talking about the National Defense Authorization Act (NDAA) passed in December 2011 and again in 2012, which contains provisions that allow for the use of the U.S. military to unlawfully detain American citizens (under the law of war) on suspicion and without charge for their potential associations with so-called terrorists without a trial or evidence thereto. Even great legal scholars, like Judge Andrew Napolitano, see this act as an assault on the U.S. Constitution for which many men and women in the military have fought and died.

In fact, a case was filed in 2012 by *New York Times* reporter Christopher Hedges. He and other journalists contend that the controversial section of the NDAA allows for the indefinite military detention of citizens by the US military "on suspicion of providing substantial support" to anyone engaged in hostilities against the United States. But the lawsuit points out that the law is vague, lacking specificity, and could be interpreted to authorize the detainment and arrest of people whose speech or associations are protected by the First Amendment. They point out, would a journalist speaking with an al-Qaida or persons knowing of al-Qaida members constitute "substantial support"? A trial judge issued a permanent injunction preventing application of sections 1021 and 1022 of the NDAA, but the case is pending before an appeals court as of this writing.

One can only surmise that the platform Paul promoted of eliminating the national debt by the end of his first term as president would have probably occurred. Look at how the other GOP presidential contenders, who dropped out of the presidential race for the nomination, racked up major campaign debts while Paul's campaign ran an efficient, cost-effective campaign with a surplus. According to Federal Election Commission (FEC) reports alluded to in an October 2012 news account, Paul's presidential campaign had more than $2 million on hand after the national GOP convention, going the full stretch up to Tampa as Romney's sole contender. Other contenders like Gingrich owed $5 million, Santorum owed more than $1 million, Bachmann owed $607,218, Herman Cain owed $175,000, Huntsman had almost $5.3

---

[11] "Video: Living under drones," http://www.dailypaul.com, http://youtu.be/6yMOzvmgVhc, September 27, 2012.

million owed.[12] All of these candidates had halted their campaigns way earlier than Paul, whose campaign ended after Tampa.

This book is intended to provide a capsule, bird's-eye view, highlighting some developments of the 2012 presidential campaign. As a citizen who read and followed the unraveling story of this presidential campaign from the sidelines, I wanted to keep it as brief and concise as possible, making it easier for the reader to absorb the core points. I am sure that there were additional occurrences that unfolded, also, that are not covered in this book. The book's observations, findings and facts, however, have strong implications for national politics and policy, the need for every American to educate themselves on issues beyond mainstream media and to become involved with the political process in some form or fashion so that the American people can regain control over their own government, returning our system to "a government for and by the people." It certainly raises the question of "who controls?" The people or elite interests, whose financial contributions impact on party selection of candidates, the path along the way to the nomination, and, inevitably, the final victor of the presidential campaign. The super-PACs, indeed, pumped excessive amounts of funding into the 2012 presidential campaign.

Despite the fact that Ron Paul did not win the Republican presidential nomination due to the Party's unfair and deceptive practices and rule changes, Paul's message attracted and inspired so many people, including America's youth, because he challenged the status quo and government's increased role in all of our lives, something which needs to be changed. In those nations experiencing tremendous economic turmoil and which had, along the way, challenges to their own freedoms, citizens abroad have come to admire the immovable principles of Ron Paul and perceived him as the presidential candidate who indeed presented real differences among those candidates running for the 2012 U.S. presidential bid. In fact, a petition was circulated and signed by thousands of individuals, calling on the Norwegian Parliament to nominate Dr. Ron Paul for the Nobel Peace prize in recognition of his efforts in promoting peace worldwide. Many felt that the power of Dr. Paul and the movement he inspired should be recognized by a Nobel Peace Prize, notwithstanding the fact that in recent

---

12    Chris Dixon, "The Republican primary legacy: debt hypocrisy (minus Ron Paul)," Banghor Daily News, http://www.banghordailynews.com, October 19, 2012.

past years, its selections have not mirrored the ideals and traits for which the award was initially established. It should be noted that despite the mainstream media's dismissive attitude concerning Dr. Paul's presidential candidacy, *Time* magazine, in its April 30, 2012, issue, named Ron Paul among one of the 100 Most Influential People in the World.

I wrote this book in my spare time from a citizen's perspective. I want to share the information I have read and collected during 2012-2013 with my fellow citizens since many individuals may not have read or heard about all of these occurrences from the corporate mainstream media.

The events that occurred and which are reported in this book are eye openers. Anomalies and alleged fraud in the early primaries and caucuses, rule abuses at state conventions, and abrupt rule changes and deceptive practices at the national Republican convention should raise the consciousness of all Americans. These developments certainly underscore how important it is to not fall prey to the messaging of the political establishment and mainstream media. The outcomes of the GOP presidential nomination process should alarm every American and should serve as a call to action for all.

It is truly a citizen's account. Regardless of your own views, political positions, and ideological leanings, I hope this account triggers your vigilance and participation at all levels of government—local, state, and national. This book commemorates the victories of Dr. Ron Paul and all of the regular, grassroots people who helped him amass delegates despite the establishment's roadblocks and use of the machinery of rules to halt the final victory—the GOP nomination for president. Those national and state party structures were aided and abetted by a media that did not provide proper or appropriate coverage of his campaign, thereby preventing the national electorate from knowing truly about the depth and scope of his platform and positions, which were clearly very different from all of the other presidential candidates, including the president of the United States. Paul's most amicable traits were his honesty, commitment to constitutional principles and unwavering integrity illustrated throughout his long congressional career and his bids for the presidency.

On November 6, 2012, the American people lost the opportunity of having a real choice of candidates for the presidency. The GOP presidential nomination process and events that preceded the 2012 presidential general election between Romney and Obama precluded any real chance for the American people to change the direction of

DEBORAH K. SMARTH

the country in a positive way, returning and saving the republic as the Founding Fathers had envisioned America. Paul's victories at state conventions in several states were stolen along the way to Tampa and then at the national convention in Tampa. The last standing presidential candidate against Romney, Ron Paul, who met the minimum threshold of five states' plurality of delegates to have his name put in nomination, was denied that opportunity due to the national RNC rule changes at the Tampa convention. The rules that were in effect at the time of the 2012 state GOP conventions and the start of the national convention in August 2012 were deliberately changed to ensure that Romney would proceed as the unquestionable GOP presidential nominee. The conditions that played out during the nomination process and at the Tampa convention prevented the American people from having the opportunity to cast their vote for a candidate whose platform paved a new path for America, a president who would embark on critically needed economic and foreign policy changes as well as restoring liberties and abiding by the principles of the U.S. Constitution. The one presidential candidate, Ron Paul, who could have begun restoring America to its former stature, was not officially on the national election ballot, although many, many voters decided that writing in his name for president was the only moral and principled vote to cast.

# CHAPTER ONE

# Winning the Delegates

PRIOR TO THE GOP county, district, and state conventions, there were the Republican primaries and caucuses. There were many anomalies in the early primary and caucus states' voting outcomes. For example, in the January 2012 Iowa GOP caucus, the Des Moines Register and the official Caucus website informed us that the official results can "never be certified" because in at least eight different precincts, there were missing votes and changing stories invalidating those precincts' results. If you recall, in Iowa, the first victor was Romney; then a while after that proclamation, it was Santorum. Instead of the initial 122,255 votes that the Iowa's party establishment cited, they amended that count to 121,503 people voting. But it was the first time in Iowa history that the Republican Party decided to change the final count to a new secret location for security reasons. This shocked many Iowans as it was tradition to see the final results calculated and announced openly at the party headquarters in Des Moines for the public at large. Later on, it surfaced that "131 different precincts reported inaccurate results" leading to certain party officials stepping down in disgrace. Even with all these anomalies, Ron Paul had a very close third finish, but the media reported as if only two candidates were involved and disregarded Paul's strong showing.

The *Examiner* reported, "What played out as a result was a mockery of democracy as Iowa election officials permanently skewed the results of the caucus, illegally miscounting and completely dismissing votes for Ron Paul, many of which were ironically from precincts that Romney lost in 2008." It was also reported that other missing or uncounted votes came from major populated areas and college town precincts which were expected to draw heavy support for Ron Paul.[13] In fact, national news coverage for this caucus had Paul leading or in a dead heat "for much of the first part of the evening." Early entrance/exit polls had Paul in first place. But somehow those showings in exit polls didn't transcribe into votes as those areas where his showings in exit polls were strongest happened to be those precincts where votes were missing and not counted. Did the media raise questions? Or was anything done by the powers to be concerning these election anomalies? Absolutely nothing happened as a follow-up to the course of events. Yet our government and elected officials always voice their opinions on elections in faraway places that may not follow the rule of law!

In Nevada, known as the Libertarian leaning state and where Dr. Paul had been organizing since 2008, a similar turn of events occurred as in Iowa. Precincts across Nevada were showing mismatched voting numbers, missing votes, and ultimately unverifiable results. Like Iowa, presidential candidate Ron Paul was polling very well. In fact, CNN was reporting in a late evening vote count that Paul won a populated Las Vegas precinct by almost 60 percent, and statistics were indicating a potential, large win for Paul. CNN had videotaped a situation whereby a Paul supporter was prevented from entering this precinct count premises to witness a fair results count.

As the voting outcomes for Ron Paul doubled in almost every state he competed in since his 2008 presidential bid, it is hard to believe that in a state grounded with Paul support, he came in third behind Romney and Gingrich. The *Nevada Sun* broke the story that Nevada GOP chairwoman Amy Tarkanian filed her resignation the next morning, following the caucus, "as obvious and rampant, widespread election fraud is sweeping through the country in an establishment elite attempt to hide the real results, in favor of a pre-chosen candidate, despite the wishes of the American people."[14]

On February 11, when the Maine Caucus was held, it appeared that a preceding week of chaos unfolded. The GOP party leaders were found to have excluded and miscounted votes, ignoring entire counties and

---

[13]   Jeffrey Phelps, "Iowa vote fraud official," http://www.examiner.com, January 21, 2012.

[14]   Jeffrey Phelps, "Nevada vote fraud official," http://www.examiner.com, February 7, 2012.

precincts, postponed specific precinct caucusing entirely, and determining which counties and precincts will and will not eventually be counted.[15]

Paul's campaign had invested a large amount of campaign resources in Maine. Party officials there decided to cancel voting in Washington County due to the threat of a snow storm. The move was perceived as a means to prevent a Paul campaign surge since the Washington county caucus represented a strong base of Paul support. Paul campaign manager, John Tate, said, "In Washington County—where Ron Paul was incredibly strong—the caucus was delayed until the following week just so the votes wouldn't be reported by the national media, purposely killing any momentum we would have had by the win."

It turned out that a prediction of three to four inches of snow that actually proved to be a dusting was enough justification for a local GOP official to postpone the caucuses so the results wouldn't be reported expediently. The GOP state chairman, Charlie Webster, announced in Portland that Romney had won 39 percent (2,190 votes) of the caucus vote with Ron Paul 36 percent (1,996). The Maine GOP published results, however, that did not include votes "from another 200 cities and towns . . . . The totals, however, only reflected about 84 percent of the state's precincts."[16]

There was an outcry from Paul supporters and those who felt disenfranchised which pushed the media and state GOP officials that all caucuses in Maine should occur and all votes be counted.

The Washington County voters were "roughly triple the number who gathered in 2008." While Paul received the majority of their votes (163) to Romney's (80), Santorum's (57), and Gingrich (4), in the end, Romney held a 156-vote advantage in the Maine statewide caucus totals. Even though Maine was another state where these votes did not determine the delegates that would be sent to the national convention, the results prevented Paul from getting a win, helping "Romney stanch the narrative of four consecutive losses."

The entrance of GOP presidential candidates, like Rick Santorum and Newt Gingrich, into the primaries and caucuses also served to further split the Conservative vote in these contests despite the fact that they were considered to be "fake" Conservatives and the Paul campaign

---

[15]   Jeffrey Phelps, "Maine vote fraud official," http://www.examiner.com, February 22, 2012.

[16]   Ibid.

took every opportunity to indicate how they were "flip-floppers" and/ or "fake Conservatives." They were able to draw votes away from Paul. Had Paul's contests been direct one-on-one races with Romney, the Conservative vote would have aligned with Paul since he was a true fiscal Conservative and a traditional Republican Conservative with regard to his non-interventionist views concerning foreign policy and military engagements. Ironically, *Bloomberg Businessweek*, in March 2013, reported about how Gingrich and Santorum were actually talking about a potential "unity ticket" prior to the Michigan Republican primary in an attempt to topple Romney. Discussion between the two campaigns began in early February 2012. Gingrich "proposed that both men join forces but remain in the race, each concentrating on the states where he matched up best against Romney."[17] A chief strategist of Santorum indicated that the Santorum campaign was trying to persuade Gingrich "to drop out and endorse Santorum." As reported, Gingrich believed he earned top ticket placement while Santorum felt he had won more states, and thus he should lead the ticket. Those differing opinions prevented the emergence of a unity ticket.

While the voters were led to believe that the results of the early primaries and caucuses were the only outcomes that counted, the Paul campaign was focused on its "delegate strategy," knowing that without the establishment's support or the media's proper coverage, it would not have the massive resources to effectively compete. So it invested its resources in a more targeted manner in those states where delegate support could be maximized. That approach led to many successes at Republican state conventions across the country.

The Paul campaign was well aware of Warren G. Harding's entry into the 1920 Republican nomination convention with fewer delegates on his side than others still on the ballot. Yet he ended up capturing the nomination and swept into the White House. Paul's campaign pursued the delegate strategy in the hope of a come-from-behind win for their candidate despite the tough odds.

"Though Ron Paul's 2012 campaign has been consistently underestimated, much as his 2008 campaign was, he has managed to continue to bring in millions of dollars in donations and to pack his rallies

---

[17]  Joshua Green, "The secret Gingrich-Santorum 'unity ticket' that nearly toppled Romney," Bloomberg Businessweek, http://www.businessweek.com, March 22, 2013.

DEBORAH K. SMARTH

with thousands of vociferous supporters." "He may not be winning the votes of entire states like Mitt Romney, but he is winning over individual delegates to the nominating convention . . ."[18]

To his credit, Paul hired well-known historian Doug Wead, who served as a senior advisor in the administration of President George Herbert Walker Bush. Wead understood the delegate process and advised accordingly throughout the many months in early 2012, where county and district conventions would lead to state GOP conventions for delegates. Despite the fact that the major media wasn't covering the stories, presidential candidate Ron Paul and his campaign were waging battles for delegates support at individual state conventions.

The campaign's extensive grassroots campaign was able to wage a truly effective effort, especially in states like Alaska, Colorado, Iowa, Louisiana, Oklahoma, Maine, Missouri, Massachusetts, Michigan, Minnesota, Nevada, Virginia, and Washington. In some instances, the Ron Paul supporters were able to win chair and vice chair spots within the Republican state committees. For example, Paul backers in Alaska were elected as party chairman and cochairman; however, they did not succeed in changing the rules to enable Paul to receive twenty-four delegates, instead he received half a dozen. The *Anchorage Daily News* reported that "at the convention, the pro-Paul convention crowd was so boisterous that U.S. Senator Lisa Murkowski—a supporter of presumed GOP nominee Mitt Romney—couldn't give her planned speech on Friday."

Despite finishing third in the Iowa caucuses, Paul supporters represented a majority in the Iowa Republican state central committee, which yielded him a majority of state convention delegates. As reported on June 16, 2012, by Fox News.com, Ron Paul won twenty-one of twenty-five delegates in Iowa to the national convention. At the district conventions, Paul won eleven of twelve delegates, and at the Saturday state convention, Paul won ten of thirteen delegates. Paul campaign chairman said of the Iowa win, "This win is a real validation for our campaign and its many supporters in Iowa and across our great nation."[19]

---

18  Connor Adams Sheets, "Ron Paul 2012: Can he beat Mitt Romney now that Newt Gingrich is bowing out?", International Business Times, http://www.ibtimes.com, April 25, 2012.

19  "Ron Paul wins 21 of 25 delegates elected in Iowa," Fox News, http://www.foxnews.com, June 16, 2012.

"It's not just Iowa Republicans or other state parties that are starting to worry. The national Republican Party is perking up and starting to take notice." *Las Vegas Sun* chief political writer, John Ralston, remarked that the "RNC appears to fear Paul supporters taking Romney slots and then not abiding by GOP rules to vote for the presumptive nominee on the first ballot in Tampa." [20]

As Doug Wead's blog noted, "It turns out that Mitt Romney and other Republican operatives were apparently very much aware of what was going on at the precinct, county, district and state conventions. This was not greedy state and county chairmen wanting to hang onto power so they could go to the RNC as delegates and get drunk. The hardball tactics were apparently approved and refined from state to state from Iowa, where the state chairman got money for the GOP and promises and conveniently kept a Santorum popularity vote win and a Ron Paul delegate win, out of the news for months, all the way to Tampa . . ."

In Minnesota's state convention held on May 19, 2012, Ron Paul swept at-large delegates by winning thirty-two of the state's forty delegates. In April, Colorado's state delegate count, Paul had the majority with eighteen delegates. It was reported by Ron Paul forces that it took the state Republican Party three days—after locking up the delegate names—to release the names of its twenty-nine delegates, and twenty-six of them were for Romney, three for Paul. However, Ron Paul convention participants and supporters noted that what was most stunning about this announcement is that at the convention itself, Paul supporters had confirmed eleven of eighteen delegates were Paul's. They questioned what happened during that three-day period before the final delegate count was issued.

In the lead-up to the state conventions, Paul was making headway. Even in states like Pennsylvania and Rhode Island, Paul was winning delegates, five and four respectively. In Minnesota, Paul won twenty of the twenty-four delegates in April district caucuses. In Boone County, Missouri, Paul received forty-eight of fifty-three delegates, and an active supporter of Paul said, "We've been working for this for four years. All of our team's work paid off today. It was peaceful and we brought in hundreds of new Ron Paul supporters to the Republican Party to work for

---

[20] Jon Ward, "Ron Paul racks up delegates, putting GOP Establishment on edge," Huffington Post, http://www.huffingtonpost.com, May 3, 2012.

the Constitution." [21] In the May Virginia congressional district caucuses, Paul was reported as taking seventeen of thirty-three delegates compared to Romney's sixteen with the final sixteen delegates to be determined in June. It was reported June 17, 2012, on the Daily Paul.com that Virginia will send twenty-five Ron Paul supporters out of forty-nine delegates to the national convention.

GOP contender Rick Santorum, who had some initial victories in the early 2012 primaries and caucuses due to intense press and media bumps provided to him, "had accused Paul of shilling for Romney" and acknowledged during an interview with Piers Morgan that "Ron Paul is working the delegates hard."[22] Paul's delegates were organized and disciplined, educated about state party and convention rules.

"Despite staunch opposition from the state Republican Party, Paul took twenty of the forty delegates awarded in Missouri (in April)," according to campaign chairman Jesse Benton. "In at least five other states—Colorado, Nevada, Iowa, Washington, and Maine—Paul has done remarkably well at county and district conventions, and his supporters are expected to win a big chunk of RNC delegates at the state conventions later this spring."[23]

Even in Missouri, where Brent Stafford—a Ron Paul supporter—won a county GOP chairman post in St. Charles, games unfolded there. Doug Wead's blog indicates that Stafford was arrested and hauled off to jail by off-duty police hired by the Romney people. He, of course, "was acquitted and the Romney person who ordered the arrest actually applauded the court's decision."

In Louisiana, unbelievable conditions played out at that state GOP convention on June 1 to 2 in Shreveport. Paul supporters dominated the caucuses in Louisiana as reported by the *New Orleans Times-Picayune*, winning four of six congressional districts with a tie in a fifth, which purported that almost three quarters of the state's convention delegates would be Paul backers. Ron Paul's campaign leadership strategists stated that the Paul camp won a majority of the delegates from Louisiana

---

[21]  "Boone County, Mo Caucus results are a solid win for RP 48 of 53 delegates," Posted on http://www.DailyPaul.com, March 17, 2012.

[22]  Grace Wyler, "Actually, Ron Paul is secretly winning a lot more delegates than you think," Business Insider, http://www.businessinsider.com, April 27, 2012.

[23]  Ibid.

to the national convention and succeeded in electing one of their own supporters to a senior party position. At the convention itself, this Paul supporter became embroiled in a dispute with other Republican Party regulars. There were also subsequent challenges to the number of delegates won by the Paul supporters. Hamdan Azhar, a Ron Paul supporter, blogged, many months later, that he experienced firsthand the difficulties at the Louisiana GOP state convention. He noted that "many of us were blocked out of proceedings and even assaulted and arrested. But it is important to note that in spite of these difficulties, or perhaps even because of them, we have gained ground."

Several months after the Louisiana convention, Doug Wead noted in his blog, "Remember how Romney-Santorum people hired off-duty policemen, telling them to arrest troublemakers when they pointed them out? And then after they were voted out and new Ron Paul people were voted in to run the convention, they had the hired off-duty policeman arrest the new duly elected chairman who was manhandled. One was knocked to the ground; another had his fingers broken while in police custody. Well, that is going to court. Yes, the Ron Paul victims will win, but the Romney people could care less; they got what they wanted and no apology has been offered."

In an August 13, 2012, communication by Paul campaign manager, John Tate, he noted, "In Louisiana, establishment 'big wigs' used threats, intimidation, and force—literally smashing the bones of one gentleman—to shut out Ron Paul supporters who had a clear majority at the State Convention."

Of the approximately 180 delegates attending the Louisiana state convention, 113 voted to remove the GOP chairman when he was not responsive to requests for information and other delegates' motions. Almost two-thirds of the delegates turned their back on the GOP chair appointed by the party hierarchy. A Paul supporter, Alex Helwig, chairman of the Rules Committee, who called for the removal of the chair, was arrested by Shreveport police and then released. When he returned to the event, it was apparent some of his fingers were broken, and he was walking with a cane. Henry Herford Jr. of Franklin Parrish, another Paul supporter who was the state central committeeman, was attacked by some security officials who didn't realize that the body voted out the previous chair. Mr. Herford was beginning to call to order the newly reformed convention. His prosthetic hip was dislocated as a result of the assault. Despite these circumstances, the convention reportedly

DEBORAH K. SMARTH

elected a slate of 27 Ron Paul delegates to fill district and at-large delegate slots to the national convention.[24]

The State party had attempted to enact last-minute rules to keep Paul's backers in check. Responding to these tactics, "Mr. Paul's fans likened the state party and Chairman Roger Villere as 'more characteristic of a North Korean politburo than a democratic American political party that honors procedures and majority votes.'" Interestingly, the state party had a brief filed accusing "Paul supporters of trying to 'hijack' the convention and overrule the will of 200,000 primary voters [in March 2012]."[25]

The Ron Paul campaign issued a statement on the Louisiana GOP convention which read: "The Ron Paul campaign condemns the unfortunate activities that took place at the Louisiana Republican State Convention in Shreveport . . . The unnecessary conflict, and positive conclusion as we understand it, transpired as follows. The LAGOP officials ignored the vast majority of duly elected delegates and attempted to use illegally adopted rules to deny Ron Paul supporters an opportunity to attend the Republican National Convention in Tampa. Louisiana has 46 delegates. Five were pledged to Mitt Romney based on the March 23 primary result and Rick Santorum received 10, meaning most delegates were contestable at the state convention."

At the same time that the Louisiana state GOP convention was taking place, the Washington state GOP convention was also occurring June 1 to 2 in Tacoma. It was reported that Ron Paul won the majority of Washington's delegates to the national convention, following victories in Iowa and Minnesota, "pointing to a hectic convention in which Mitt Romney's path to the nomination may face a major insurgent opponent."[26] Victories at state conventions were mounting.

---

24    Hamdan Azhar, PolicyMic, http://www.policymic.com/articles/9163/Louisiana-convention-results-ron-paul-delegates-arrested-as-they-command-majority, June 3, 2012.

25    David Sherfinski, "Ron Paul backers fight effectively for GOP goals," Washington Times,http://www.washingtontimes.com/news/2012/aug/8/its-not-over-till-its-over-for-backers-of-Ron-Paul, August 8, 2012.

26    Connor Adams Sheets, "Ron Paul 2012 wins majority of Washington delegates to convention, other states expected to follow," International Business Times, http://www.ibtimes.com, April 26, 2012.

In Nevada, despite the fact that Romney took 50 percent of Nevada caucus goers in February and Paul took 19 percent, the actual GOP Nevada state convention was held on May 5, 2012, in Sparks, Nevada. Ron Paul won a majority of the state's delegates to the party's national convention through the hard work of organized Paul supporters; twenty-two of the twenty-five Nevada delegates were Paul supporters.[27]

Longtime Nevada political columnist Jon Ralston commented that "the Paul folks couldn't get their people turned out for the caucus. But, they outmaneuvered the Nevada Romney people ever since and dominated the county conventions and this is the inevitable result." It should be noted that the Paul supporters had better planned and prepared since his 2008 presidential bid. While the regular-party Republicans tried to shut down the convention in 2008, when Paul supporters tried to elect their own delegates, the 2012 bid prevented the Romney supporters from blocking Paul delegates this time.

In addition, both the Republican National committeeman and committeewoman from Nevada, Bob List and Heidi Smith, were ousted in landslides to James Smack and Diana Orrick, both supporters of Ron Paul. In fact, it was apparent that the Republican National Committee, which wanted to move ahead with an "uneventful" (choreographed) national convention, was seeing Paul supporters in different states win delegate majorities. Tim Morgan, an attorney from California who had served as a GOP national committeeman for a dozen years, came to the Nevada convention at the request of the RNC national counsel. In his own words, as reported in a press account, Morgan said to a Nevada delegate to "make sure you don't do anything to jeopardize your national delegates."[28] The impression by many was that the RNC Counsel was sending a messenger like Morgan "to whip the Nevada Republicans into line."

Prior to the state convention, RNC's chief counsel John R. Phillippe Jr. sent a threatening letter to Nevada Republicans which evoked an angry response from them. Phillippe's communication was described in a newspaper account as "expecting the recipients to obediently kowtow."

27   Weiner, Rachel, "Ron Paul wins majority of Nevada delegates," Washington Post, http://washingtonpost.com, May 6, 2012.
28   Allan Stevo, "Ron Paul will win Nevada, despite RNC manipulation and foul play for Mitt Romney," PolicyMic, www.policymic.com/articles/7933, May 5, 2012.

DEBORAH K. SMARTH

The letter inevitably concerned the issue of voting to unbind delegates to prevent a precedent in other states' GOP conventions. It was clear throughout the long trail of state conventions and the increasing victories of Ron Paul delegates that the regular party establishment was concerned. While Paul supporters were hoping to have input into the national party platform and gain a prime-time speaking slot for the lone standing Republican presidential contender to Mitt Romney, the GOP establishment was concerned about any potential disruptions by Paul backers at the national convention. Even former presidential candidate Newt Gingrich, who dropped out of the race due to dried-up funds, expressed concerns that the strong grassroots, delegate support for Ron Paul could be the "biggest danger for Romney in Tampa."

It was reported that at a May 15 meeting of the Clark County GOP in Nevada, Paul supporters "pushed through a resolution rebuking Republican National Committee chief Reince Priebus and calling on him to resign his post due to his decision to merge some RNC fundraising with that of presumptive presidential nominee Mitt Romney." They charged that Mr. Priebus violated an RNC rule against aiding one party presidential hopeful while another presidential candidate remains in the race. A blog by Nevada political analyst Elizabeth Crum posted the Clark County Republican statement which read: "We hope that our Republican colleagues in local and state parties across the nation will join with us in expressing our outrage at having our role in the nomination process usurped by a select few individuals."

While Romney narrowly won the Maine non-binding caucus earlier in the year, Ron Paul's army of supporters succeeded in winning the majority of delegates in the state of Maine at the GOP state convention held May 5-6 at the Augusta Convention Center.[29] Even at that early juncture, party regulars who supported Romney charged that the delegation may not be seated at the national convention. Later on as the national convention drew closer, the party's actions to take away Paul delegate credentials provoked Maine governor Paul LePage's threat that he would not attend the national convention as he believed the Paul delegates won their spots according to the rules.

Prior to the Maine GOP state convention, it was reported that Republican state party chairman Charlie Webster had predicted in a

---

[29]  Associated Press, "Ron Paul wins majority of delegates from Maine GOP," May 6, 2012.

message to Republicans that the Paul supporters would try and take over the convention, referring to them as wingnuts, perceiving them as a fringe minority. But the Paul supporters succeeded in winning the majority of votes at the state convention. In fact, convention participants elected a Paul delegate as secretary and another Paul delegate as chairman of the convention. It was a painstakingly slow moving process as indicated by a state legislator from Maine who had previously attended two conventions. Representative Jeffrey Timberlake, R-Turner said, "What has taken six or seven hours today is normally done in 15 to 20 minutes," advocating for a return to a primary instead of a caucus.[30]

According to senior advisor to the Paul campaign, Doug Wead wrote in his October 18 blog that "perhaps the most damaging news of all for the Romney campaign" was the story of Charlie "The Cheater" Nejedly. According to the blog, Nejedly was wearing a Ron Paul sticker and distributing fake Ron Paul slates at the Maine GOP State Convention which Romney had clearly lost. As Wead says, "He was outed on the floor in Maine and soon afterward overheard talking to Romney's likely nominee for Attorney General, campaign legal counsel, Ben Ginsberg. According to the source, Ginsberg told Nejedly, 'We need to get you to Boston.'"

As reported by Paul campaign manager, subsequent to the Maine victory, he indicated that "the establishment is attempting to unseat the state's duly elected delegates and alternates—acting like sore losers in the process. The challenge to our delegates in Maine is so bogus that Republican Governor Paul LePage—who is one of the few delegates not being challenged by the establishment—has declared he will not attend the Republican National Convention unless Ron Paul's delegates and alternates who were duly elected are seated."

Quite unique developments occurred at the May 12 Oklahoma Republican state convention, provoking legal challenges. The strength and presence of Paul supporters at the state convention illustrated itself when the "GOP Oklahoma Governor Mary Fallin was booed at the convention when she said the party's single goal was to elect Romney as president."[31]

---

[30] Eric Russell, "As predicted, Ron Paul backers take over Maine GOP convention," Banghor Daily News, http://www.banghordailynews.com, May 5, 2012.

[31] "Ron Paul convention delegates deal cut," United Press International, http:// www.upi.com/Top_News, August 21, 2012.

DEBORAH K. SMARTH

The temporary chairman of that state convention ended the convention before a roll call for delegate selection occurred, thereby rendering the adjournment illegitimate. Party state rules had stipulated that only two thirds of attendees at a convention could legally adjourn such a meeting.

Since that rule was not followed, a group of participants who felt disenfranchised continued the proceedings outside in the parking lot to continue business in a different location since scheduled business of the convention had not been completed. An Internet account clearly provided that such actions were consistent with the rules of order as the presumed leaders acted with impunity, operating outside of the rules. In fact, the temporary chair had initially asked for a voice vote rather than a roll-call vote despite objections from the floor. The chair rationalized his move by saying that "it was the way they always did it." However, party rules required a roll-call vote.

Prior to the abrupt adjournment of the convention, it was noted by bystanders and verified by a live video feed from the event (http://www.livestream.tv/channel/suriyahfish) that "the lights were immediately turned off and the walls to the convention center started to close in on the attendees." In addition, it was reported by attendees that the portable walls were rearranged in such a way that it was impossible for voters from the affected districts to vote in the ongoing process. A video aired by KFOR-TV, Oklahoma City, documented that many of the attendees were indeed isolated from the rest of the body as a result of the partitioning of the room and the lights being turned off.[32] Furthermore, others attested to the fact that Robert's Rules of Order were ignored as the party establishment pushed its agenda. Many believed that the GOP operatives attempted to orchestrate pushing their candidate, Mitt Romney, on a group of delegates who wanted to vote for Ron Paul.

As the Oklahoma convention continued in the parking lot, a convention chair was elected, overseeing proceedings with "confidence and dignity." After several hours of procedural meandering and roll-call votes—despite the fact that many participants had left earlier prior to the convening of the parking lot convention—the real slate of delegates was selected. As the convention waned, participants began cheering and chanting "Ron Paul" and "we cannot be bought." The latter statement, some believe, was in response to the fact that "the Romney campaign had repeatedly been accused of paying people to endorse the Governor and

---

[32]   Ibid.

to serve as his delegates." Preliminary estimates acknowledged that Paul had captured 95 percent of the Oklahoma delegates despite the challenges presented to Paul supporters.

The actions of the Oklahoma party organization and its party leaders "made a complete mockery of the democratic process." Those attending and familiar with Robert's Rules of Order contend that many violations occurred, such as not appointing a convention chair required by party rules, and the existing chair ignored floor motions and calls for division.[33]

As reported by the Paul campaign officials, "in Oregon, the State Chairman blatantly ignored the votes of the Convention, taking it upon himself to replace the duly elected alternate delegates with an 'appointed' slate chocked-full of establishment cronies."[34] An August 3, 2012, news account reported that in five Oregon congressional district conventions held on June 23, 2012, "Republican precinct officials supporting Paul showed up in force and held to a disciplined strategy of voting for a slate of delegates." It was reported by GOP spokesman, Greg Leo, that "he thinks the Paul forces won half of Oregon's 28 delegates to the convention." Paul's Oregon coordinator, Tom Armstrong, maintained that "his side actually has 15 of the 28 delegates."[35] Armstrong further stated that the Oregon GOP leadership and the state chairman Allen Alley "are not happy with the delegation election results. They wanted their family, friends, and 'good old boys' seated on the delegation and they're willing to break every rule and bylaw to make that happen." A precinct committee person, Kevin Renfrow, who was a duly elected alternate delegate, said, "There was an organized effort by the Oregon Party leadership to impede the proceedings of the conventions and stall for as long as possible."

The state party chairman Allen Alley reportedly shut down the district conventions at 5 p.m., just as precinct workers began selecting alternate delegates. Later on, the executive committee of the state party chose alternates who were illegitimate appointments. One of the many appointments made at a secret June 30 meeting to replace the state's duly elected alternate delegates was Ourania Yue, wife of national

---

[33] Kevin Kervick, "GOP establishment makes a mockery of the democratic process in Oklahoma," http://www.examiner.com, May 12, 2012.

[34] John Tate, "Let the Fight Begin," letter to supporters, August 13, 2012.

[35] Jeff Mapes, "Ron Paul supporters fighting for control of Oregon republican delegation to national convention," The Oregonian, http://www.oregonlive.com, August 3, 2012.

DEBORAH K. SMARTH

committeeman and executive committee member Solomon Yue. Others on the list were also people who hadn't even filed for the positions to which they were appointed.

According to information posted on DailyPaul.com on July 6, Alley sent a letter to those who thought they had been duly elected only to be told that "if you are receiving this letter, you have not been elected as a Delegate or Alternate Delegate to the Oregon Delegation for the Republican National Convention in Tampa, FL. Thank you so much for your service to our Party." The legal team representing the Ron Paul Presidential Campaign Committee sent a letter to the Oregon Republican Party concerning their attempted actions to unseat duly elected alternate delegates. An official challenge with the RNC was also filed by the Paul campaign. As a result of the kinds of activities that had occurred, a resolution to the Republican Executive Committee, the Oregon Republican Party, and the Republican National Committee was circulated to the state's hundreds of precinct committee persons who were disenfranchised and whose voting rights were violated. The resolution firmly stated that the June 30 Oregon Republican Party Executive Committee meeting was a violation of the party's bylaws and it also alluded to the failure of giving the required thirty-day written notice, etc. The role of both the delegates and alternates cannot be underestimated as they vote on the chair of the delegation to the national convention and to convention committee memberships.

The kind of occurrence at the Oregon GOP proceedings led one Washington County homemaker, Judy Morrise, who was elected on the Paul slate but who became a Romney-pledged delegate, to say, "It's just stark cronyism." She reportedly supported the Paul supporters' credentials challenge.[36]

As the nomination process unfolded, some maintained that Santorum supporters, whose candidate withdrew after some initial good showings in primaries/caucuses, joined with Paul organizers attempting to deny Romney delegates because Romney was not perceived as a Conservative. For instance, Paul campaign chairman Jesse Benton noted that there was a real anti-establishment sense in Colorado and that they believed supporters of Santorum would move toward Paul. Paul was reported as

---

[36]  Jeff Mapes, "Ron Paul supporters fighting for control of Oregon republican delegation to national convention," The Oregonian, http:// www.oregonlive. com, Oregonian, August 3, 2012.

getting thirteen delegates in Colorado during the April 14 state GOP convention. In the state of Washington, the county caucus organizer for Santorum was reported as sending an "open letter to his fellow supporters, urging them to vote for Paul's delegates rather than Romney's."

Paul senior campaign advisor, Doug Wead, indicated that the plurality of Santorum supporters just don't want to vote for Romney, and they were taking a closer look at Ron Paul, indicating that that Romney had major problems with the Republican base. News accounts noted that even though Romney may have had primary election successes, he was unable to get his delegates seated in many states where he won the primary by a wide margin. Some attributed the lackluster support to the fact that there was "a strong anti-Romney undercurrent among traditional conservatives."

Doug Wead indicates in his post-convention blog, "Remember Arizona? Where there were accusations of voter fraud and physical violence against Ron Paul delegates? Where delegates were sweated out, kept in 100 degree temperatures without air conditioning and without breaks for water or toilet, in hopes of getting them to give up?" As one participant at the Arizona convention wrote on the Daily Paul Internet site on May 14 (following the event), "Arizona's State Convention was a joke. Liberty delegates and their votes were cast aside and left out in the cold despite having a massive voting bloc. Well we are not standing for it anymore. We are passing resolutions condemning the actions of the Arizona GOP and kicking out the charlatans." The poster of the comments also shared a video "showing the people standing up against corruption."

The executive director of the Nebraska Republican Party was warned by GOP officials in Nevada and Louisiana that they should be prepared for the "Paulistas," whom they said "try to seize control of the convention through endless votes, amendments, re-votes and parliamentary delays aimed at wearing out establishment Republicans." According to an MSNBC account by NBC's Anthony Terrell, Republicans showing up at that state convention were "met with additional security, hired by the state party in anticipation of a Paul insurgency."

Nebraska Tea Party and Republican Liberty Caucus Leader Laura Ebke, pointed out that "many counties aren't sending a delegate to the convention, which ought to worry state party officials."[37] Commenting on

---

[37] Deena Winter, "Exclusive: Security heightened at GOP convention in anticipation of Ron Paul insurgency," http://www.nebraskawatchdog.org, July 6, 2012.

DEBORAH K. SMARTH

the final state GOP convention in Nebraska, Governor Dave Heineman, the first Republican governor to endorse Romney, stated to reporters after the Nebraska convention vote that the state's delegation to the national convention should coalesce with the primary outcome where Romney won by a large vote percentage.

While Paul's forces didn't win that convention, the same dedication and focus persisted. It is also interesting to note certain perceptions by those who participated. For example, it was reported by a county delegate to the Nebraska convention that although the liberty-minded folks did not have the delegates in place to win in Nebraska, "nowhere in the rules numbered 1 through 14 was there any ballot construction guidelines. The ballot in my opinion was slanted dramatically. At the top of the ballot was a framed box that stated 'it' (the nominees in this area) was the Romney slate. This framed box contained the names of those fully vetted to support 'the agenda' of Mitt Romney. Below this was a random listing of the others wishing to seek the support of the voter." The convention delegate further said that under normal circumstances, he would not have thought anything of it until he heard a sergeant of arms instructing an older gentleman that "if you support Mitt Romney you need only to vote for the candidates in the top box, the rest are other supporters." This occurrence happened during the National Convention Delegates by Congressional District election.[38]

Recognizing the insurmountable obstacles and barriers to winning a national GOP convention whose insider power base and leaders were oriented toward Romney, the Paul campaign believed that it could do everything it can "to win as many delegates" as possible. Campaign leadership was quoted as saying: "We want to have a strong, respectful presence that says 'we are here, we are going to participate, and we are ready to talk about the party platform with you if you take our issues seriously.' We're going to send a message that the liberty wing of the Republican Party is strong, and that it isn't going anywhere." So Paul's campaign efforts continued through Tampa.

"All his other fellow long-shots have dropped out. The Republican National Committee is calling former Massachusetts governor Mitt

---

[38] Comment Post on the Daily Paul by Convention Delegate, "Nebraska convention delegates biggest concern," http://www.DailyPaul.com, July 14, 2012.

Romney the 'presumptive nominee.' Yet at state conventions around the country, Paul supporters are increasing the candidate's support by taking over state party committees and educating fellow Paul fans in arcane rules."[39] Paul's supporters continued to push forward until the very end at the national convention.

Even in Romney's home state of Massachusetts, Paul succeeded in winning the majority of delegates to the national convention only later on to run up against the powerful party structure's attempts to dismantle those legitimate wins. That statewide caucus was held on April 28, 2012. As reported by the *Boston Globe*, less than half of Romney's twenty-seven chosen delegates won at the statewide caucuses. The list of losers included some big names like former lieutenant governor Kerry Healey and Massachusetts house minority leader Bradley H. Jones, Jr.[40] Prominent alternate delegates like Charles Baker and Sheriff Frank Cousins Jr. also lost.[41]

Ben Swann, Emmy award winning news reporter with Fox WXIX Cincinnati, known for his "Reality Check" report, noted that the Massachusetts delegates to the RNC in Tampa received a letter and affidavit that they are being asked to sign and return, affirming that "under the pain and penalty of perjury, they will vote for Mitt Romney in the first round of voting." The letter sent by Ed McGrath, the Allocation Committee chairman, provides that "electronic delivery, in any form, will not be accepted." It further provides that unless the affidavit is submitted on time, "your status as a delegate is in jeopardy." Swann also convincingly laid out why this demand was both verifiably illegal on different grounds on his Facebook site, www.facebook.com/BenSwann Reality Check. He further indicated that Jerry Davis at Lawyers for Ron Paul indicated the following: "It is illegal to force anyone to vote any certain way . . . period!!!; all of the binding is under civil constitutional law . . . verifiably . . . illegal . . . any means of manipulating a vote, whether by proxy or by unit, is illegal; the RNC's use of these rules in

---

[39]  Rachel Weiner, "Ron Paul's stealth state convention takeover," Washington Post, http://www.washingtonpost.com, May 2, 2012.

[40]  Connor Adams Sheets, "Ron Paul 2012 delegate strategy makes new gains in Massachusetts, Alaska," International Business Times, http://www.ibtimes. com,  April 30, 2012.

[41]  Stephanie Ebbert, "State GOP's caucus picks leave Romney slate slighted," Boston Globe, http://www.bostonglobe.com, April 30, 2012.

their very nature, are illegal . . ." Furthermore, in August 2008, an RNC Counsel memo indicated that Rule 38 meant that "no delegate or alternate delegate shall be bound by any attempt of any state or congressional district to impose the unit rule."

As reported by *Politico*, citing the *Boston Globe*, an affidavit was never mentioned in the Republican rules for selecting delegates "and has never been required of delegates in the past."[42] After having witnessed what the Massachusetts GOP did, Evan Kenney, who had just turned eighteen, registering to vote for the first time and who had campaigned to become an alternate delegate to the Republican National Convention, said, "I've been rudely awakened to the realities of politics. I feel I've been cheated." Carol Claros, a single mother from Worcester, Massachusetts, who was a nurse and who worked with other Liberty Caucus activists to increase attendance and support for the Liberty delegates, said they did it "the old-fashioned way," reaching out to Liberty voters. She said, "We must have called 2,000 people in the state. I was like a phone warrior." Brad Wyatt, a Liberty delegate organizer, reported that he was "very disappointed and disheartened about the way we've been treated. It's almost unbelievable."[43]

The same individual who had worked the Maine GOP state convention, Charlie "The Cheater" Nejedly, was an operative at the Massachusetts GOP state convention. According to Doug Wead's October 2012 blog, "he was a paid staffer on the Romney payroll."

The Massachusetts situation was described most succinctly by Paul campaign manager, John Tate, when he stated, "In Mitt Romney's home state of Massachusetts, corrupt Party officials changed the rules after the game was over—kicking out Ron Paul's duly elected delegates and alternates and replacing them with their hand-picked cronies." As reported by *GQ Magazine* on July 11, 2012, it was reported that the state party, in a statement from the chairman of the Allocation Committee, said "it was the Romney campaign's decision to bounce the 17 Paul supporters." In the end, it was decided that the dispute over affidavits was "just cause for not being certified as national delegates."

---

[42]   Alexander Burns, "Paul supporters booted in Massachusetts, Politico, http://www.politico.com/blogs/Burns-Haberman/, June 25, 2012.

[43]   Stephanie Ebbert, "Massachusetts Republicans oust Ron Paul delegates," Boston Globe, http://www.bostonglobe.com, June 24, 2012.

During a June 18 interview of an Illinois Ron Paul delegate, Greg Bishop, who attended the Illinois Republican state convention on June 9, 2012, Bishop explained how the Ron Paul delegation was shut out of the state GOP convention. The Independent Voter Project provided excerpts of the interview (Q & A with an Illinois Ron Paul Delegate: "Leadership dictates the party"). He relayed that despite being organized and in the weeks leading to the convention holding conference calls and working on platform issues, they "quickly realized that it (the platform committee) was an exclusive process" and that "we walked away feeling very disenfranchised." He stated that this particular state convention was the largest one in Illinois state history due to the involvement of the Ron Paul supporters, yet he acknowledged that as outsiders, "we don't fall in line with what the Old Guard has in mind for the future of the Republican Party." He expressed that some of the supporters felt that "getting shut out of the convention was a deliberate effort to keep the liberty message out of the Republican Party." When they tried to get a motion on the floor, it was apparent that the "leadership dictates to the lower ranks what to do and very few lower ranks diverge from that prescribed path." As Bishop explained, it was only a petition to get the motion on the floor for a vote.

It was apparent, in light of the Paul delegates at various state GOP conventions winning ground, that the party regulars and GOP leaders in other states were trying to characterize the Paul campaign and its supporters as using "disruptive tactics" at state conventions as reported in a Times-Picayune August 7, 2012, news account. But actually, when one examines all these occurrences as a whole, it is clear that the Romney and GOP operatives were hard at work, trying to undermine the advances of the Paul delegate strategy.

Despite the fact that Paul's campaign was garnering delegate gains in various states, throughout the entire campaign process, it was notable that the Associated Press continued to downplay the delegate numbers and seriously under-reported Paul's victories at state conventions. It became evident as a voter looking in from the outside that other data was needed in weighing the facts about Paul's successes, and a website known as http://thereal2012delegatecount appeared to be more reliable in terms of tracking progress for Paul, the Republican congressman with Libertarian leanings. Actually, Paul forces disputed the totals of AP reports and contended that "their candidate has far more support than the AP gives him."[44]

It was clear that the GOP establishment was worried. Alaska's longtime GOP chairman, Randy Ruedrich, commented to the *Anchorage Daily News* that Ron Paul could win the nomination despite having fewer delegates than Romney. "Under the national Republican Party rules, if a presidential candidate can secure the support of delegates from five states at the national convention, they can attempt to win the nomination even if they haven't won a single state primary or poll." Fox News even reported in April that Paul's presence on the ballot at the Republican National Convention "looks inevitable at this point."

There were so many occurrences that happened at many Republican state conventions that seemed out of the ordinary. Romney campaign officials were alleged to be distributing fake delegate slates in Maine and Nevada to confuse the process of delegate votes. Police were called in to shut down the St. Charles caucus in Missouri when a Ron Paul victory seemed imminent. Doug Wead, senior campaign adviser to the Paul campaign, in his October 19, 2012, blog even commented about "just how tough and dirty the Mitt Romney campaign fought to block the Ron Paul takeover of the Republican Party at the State Conventions."

Due to the media blackout, most voters didn't even know that Ron Paul was in the presidential race, let alone realize that he had won the majority of delegates in so many states. It sends a message to all of us about how corrupt the power structure can become and how important it is that each one of us, no matter from what walk of life we come, must band together to understand the political developments occurring daily, weekly, monthly, yearly as citizens who participate in the process. Never can we be just bystanders.

One thing is for sure and that is that Ron Paul "has won the battle of ideas. Many are moving in Paul's direction, and that is a victory larger than winning the Republican nomination."[45] Iowa State Representative Erik Helland said, "Ron Paul is the most successful presidential candidate in the last couple of decades, even though he hasn't won the election, he

---

[44]  Kenneth Walsh, "Ron Paul Snatches Half of Louisiana's Delegates," US News & World Report, http://www.usnews.com/news/blogs, June 4, 2012.

[45]  Kevin Kelly, "Ron Paul has already won," Washington Times, http://communities.washingtontimes.com, May 22, 2012.

has shaped the dialogue."[46] Despite the fact that Paul initiated discussion of issues that the political establishment preferred not to raise, there is no doubt that the message of the Liberty wing of the party is spreading.

In the aftermath of the Republican National Convention and the November presidential election, the Ron Paul delegates and supporters who helped this candidate win majorities of delegates in various, numerous states are also becoming part of the regular party organizations and taking over leadership positions in such states like Iowa, Nevada, and others. In January 2013, Iowa's state Republican governing body re-elected two of Paul's top 2012 caucus aides to chairman and vice chairman slots. The same occurred in Nevada as Paul supporters took the two spots on the Republican National Committee.

In Minnesota, the chief organizer of Paul supporters, Marianne Stebbins, controls the Liberty wing of the Republican Party and will inevitably wield influence among the party's grassroots faction who will determine the contest for a new Republican chairman in Minnesota. As she points out, "These folks are still very active and working together, meeting and discussing organization." The Ron Paul supporters will make efforts to take control of the Minnesota state central committee.[47] She is quick to underscore that the litmus test for future candidates receiving support from the Liberty wing of the Republican Party revolves around principles. She stated, "We are not interested in electing any Republican that runs. We want to choose a candidate that has principles." Even though Paul's candidate for the U.S. Senate, high school teacher Kurt Bills, lost to establishment GOP candidate Amy Klobuchar, the Liberty wing is sure to underscore that he started his campaign late and the establishment Republicans ran his campaign.

Also, Paul backers continue to make inroads in Colorado, Florida, Louisiana, Maine, Minnesota, and Missouri, building on the work of his 2012 presidential bid.[48] The commitment to real Conservative and Libertarian principles catalyzes Paul supporters to continue their

---

[46] Jon Ward, "Ron Paul racks up delegates, putting GOP establishment on edge," Huffington Post, http://www.huffingtonpost.com, May 3, 2012.

[47] Cyndy Brucato, "Minnesota GOP will choose new state chair from rival factions still at war," http://www.minnpost.com, January 14, 2013.

[48] Thomas Beaumont, "Ron Paul's Republican legacy growing in caucus states like Iowa and Nevada," Associated Press, http://www.huffingtonpost.com, January 15, 2013.

participation and involvement in the political process and Republican Party activities.

While Congressman Paul did not seek re-election to Congress and retired from Congress in January 2013, his followers won House seats in Florida, Georgia, Kentucky, Michigan, and Texas last year. Due to the failed Romney candidacy in the November presidential election, national Republican Party leaders are now only realizing the importance of attracting the Paul youth voters and other grassroots leaders in the Paul army. It was noted that exit polls during the November election indicated that Obama had a higher percentage of younger voters (under forty-five) in contrast to Romney, 50 percent versus 40 percent.

It is known that Ron Paul drew very large crowds—in the thousands—while campaigning on college campuses across the country, and he carried a higher percentage of younger voters than Romney. The young voters are embracing Paul's message and his positions such as smaller government and no foreign entanglements that can lead to undeclared wars. Ron Paul brought the youngest delegation in the history of the Republican Party to the national convention in Tampa, August 2012. But one story which was covered by the *Daily Caller* reported that even on college campuses—which is where students and youth would flock to Paul's campus speeches—the establishment occasionally presented roadblocks. One such occurrence related to a young student, Eric Philips, at Auburn University in Alabama, who hung a Ron Paul poster in his window, just as he had seen other students do to show their support for President Obama and other causes during his time at the college. Within three hours of putting up the Paul sign, he was told by campus authorities that he needed to take it down for so-called safety reasons. But after he was told to remove the sign, ironically, reportedly around campus, there were other window hangings left up. The local media and John Stossel of Fox News, shed light on the story as it touched upon the issue of "free speech." "It wasn't hard to demonstrate that he (Eric Philips) had been singled out."[49]

Had the corporate media provided the Paul platform with better levels of coverage, the dynamic in the primary elections and smaller caucus elections, prior to the Republican state conventions, most likely

---

[49] Greg Lukianoff, "Unlearning Liberty: Auburn's censorship of Ron Paul poster is part of a larger problem," The Daily Caller, http://dailycaller.com, September 20, 2012.

would have drawn a greater level of electoral knowledge and ultimately, potentially increased voter support than what Paul actually received. Even though he effectively placed strong second and third places among the initial eight presidential Republican contenders in such primary and caucus states, the GOP establishment and the corporate media were two major barriers and obstacles for Paul to pull out major wins. However, it is interesting to note that in the Virginia two-candidate primary race, where Romney outspent Paul and had greater campaign resources with the support of a Republican governor and party establishment, Ron Paul drew 40 percent of the popular vote. The corporate media hardly discussed this good showing or did they provide access to the story of Paul's almost first place in the Maine caucuses, where it was cited later—on the Internet and in state media reports—that GOP caucus voting anomalies included the transposition of numbers in vote tallies and the denial of votes in those counties where Paul's support was highest.

Despite the GOP establishment's maneuvering rules at state conventions and sending in the so-called operatives, Paul amazingly showed that his grassroots support at these important official gatherings led to some phenomenal majority victories, sending an army of Paul supporters as delegates to the Republican National Convention in Tampa in August 2012.

# CHAPTER TWO

# On to Tampa: The Republican National Convention

AUTHOR AND POLITICAL analyst for Fox News channel Juan Williams wrote in his column, "If you have not been paying attention, it is time to look around and realize that we are living in the political age of Representative Ron Paul." Williams attributed that the victory of the GOP in the 2010 House of Representatives election "grew largely out of the ashes of Paul's 2008 presidential campaign" which emphasized limited government and a return to constitutional principles. His 2012 bid continued this mantra.

Referring to the Ron Paul Liberty movement on its way to the national convention, Dave Cushman, a new GOP state central committee member from Iowa, summed it up perfectly. He told the *Des Moines Register* that "the movement has a huge responsibility when it goes to Tampa . . . to show we are a real movement and we are not there to be rabble-rousers. The goal is not to embarrass the party. The goal is to make the party stronger and broaden the base, and walk the Republican talk."[50]

While those headed to Tampa took their political and civic role seriously, the GOP welcomed them by having their Ron Paul signs confiscated. But little did the Paul supporters know that this was just the beginning of other tactics to come. Despite the obstacles along the way, the Ron Paul delegates and supporters were only interested in promoting what they considered the best solutions to improve America's current standing; they felt strongly that their candidate's ideas and the movement

---

50 "Ron Paul wins 21 of 25 delegates elected in Iowa," Fox News, http://www. foxnews.com, June 16, 2012.

he catalyzed deserved appropriate recognition. They wanted to press the flesh and engage with other Conservatives participating at the convention as well as the media concerning the strong positions of their presidential candidate, Ron Paul.

As Paul himself said, the "establishment hasn't just sat still and quietly watched us take over party chapters and rack up delegates." He referred to the convention as "our opportunity to plant our flag and show that our Liberty movement is the future of the GOP." In a June 2012 video, Paul said to his loyal followers, "We should not be disruptive, but should also not be pushed around and that to me is very, very important." In addition, Paul continued to raise funds up to the convention so that Liberty delegates who could not afford lodging and travel to Tampa would be assisted by the campaign. In addition, as Paul acknowledged a month before the national convention, "We're expecting a credentials battle at the convention to ensure the national GOP doesn't just 'look the other way' at some of the dirty tricks my supporters had to deal with in many states."[51] Despite these occurrences, Paul's supporters made their presence known in Tampa.

Loyal supporters of Ron Paul of Texas were "still fighting a rear-guard—and effective—battle for delegates at the state level with just weeks to go before Republicans gather for their national convention in Tampa, Florida." In fact, just a few weeks prior to the convention, a federal judge allowed Paul delegates "to file an amended complaint in a case in which they accuse the Republican National Committee of manipulating the delegate allocation process."[52] A group of Paul supporters, Lawyers for Paul, working without the support of the official Paul campaign, filed a federal lawsuit in advance of the convention in the hope of getting "the Republican National Committee to admit that no delegate is 'bound' to vote for Romney." They evidently hoped that such a declaration would leave the possibility open for a Paul surprise victory at the national convention.[53] As the former national political director of Rick

---

[51]  Jennifer Harper, "Inside the Beltway: Ron Paul is not done yet," Washington Times, http://www.washingtontimes.com, July 31, 2012.

[52]  David Sherfinski, "Ron Paul backers fight effectively for GOP goals," Washington Times, http://www.washingtontimes.com/2012/aug/8/its-not-over-till-its-over-for-backers-of-ron-paul, August 8, 2012.

[53]  Brian Doherty, "Ron Paul's delegate fight with the GOP," Reason Magazine, http://reason.com/archives, August 1, 2012.

DEBORAH K. SMARTH

Santorum's campaign, Andrew Boucher stated, concerning the delegates and state conventions, that "this entire system rewards people who show up, and what we learned through the state convention processes is that Ron Paul's organization has been showing up . . . But, in doing so, as these various delegation fights prove, they've been butting heads with the party's entrenched powers."[54]

It was clear that "the Republican National Convention in Tampa, Florida . . . will be a carefully scripted show promoting Mitt Romney for president, but the Ron Paul supporters who dominate the Minnesota delegation plan to do some improvising to shift a bit of the spotlight to their libertarian cause."[55] As Marianne Stebbins, the chairwoman of the Minnesota delegation who happened to manage Paul's campaign in Minnesota earlier in 2012, said, "We want to ensure that it's known that liberty people are here, we're growing, and we're not going away." She also noted that "the Romney campaign is keeping very tight control of what's going to go on there. They have not been terribly open to bringing us in."

At the inception of the RNC's Platform Committee deliberations, Virginia governor Bob McDonnell, the chairman, said, "This is grass-roots democracy, I think, at its finest and urged the 112 delegates to 'be passionate but civil, recognizing that our goal is to have a united Republican Party.'" As reported in media accounts, Paul "delegates are making a diligent effort to wedge the defeated presidential candidate's libertarian ideas into the party document. Among them: Curbing the power of the Federal Reserve, enhancing the constitutional rights of individuals and opposing the overseas role of U.S. military forces."[56] The month prior to the convention, Paul was quoted as saying that they anticipated a possible "battle over a plank opposing the so-called Patriot Act and undeclared wars." In addition, his other key issues focused on Internet freedom, an audit of the Federal Reserve, and preventing "the indefinite detention of American citizens" under the NDAA.

At a drafting session of the committee, Linda Bean, an L.L. Bean heiress from Maine who was also a Paul delegate, asked that language be inserted concerning the role of the United States military overseas and

---

[54] Ibid.

[55] Bill Salisbury, "Many Minnesota delegates carry Ron Paul's message to RNC in Tampa," http://www.TwinCities.com, August 25, 2012.

[56] Paul West, "Ron Paul delegates taking aim at Republican Party Platform," Los AngelesTimes, http://www.latimes.com, August 20, 2012.

foreign engagement activities.[57] Pastor Kevin Erickson of Mountain Iron, Minnesota, another Paul delegate, pushed for Paul's issues on the platform committee, and he noted that the Paul forces had won and lost some issues and that it was a fair process. The platform did endorse Dr. Paul's position of better monitoring the Federal Reserve Bank monetary policies, but the committee did not condemn the National Defense Authorization Act (NDAA) that allows for indefinite military detention of any suspected terrorist, including U.S. citizens, without due process. Concerning the national party platform, it was reported that "the Paul campaign was pleased with the tough language in the platform regarding the Federal Reserve and a willingness to at least allow a public discussion on other issues even if they were not adopted."[58] However, some suggested that the party tried to appease Paul supporters regarding the platform. The committee issued "empty promises to convene another gold commission, and included a vague doctrine on Internet freedom." In addition, Senator Jim Talent, a Romney surrogate, fought efforts by the Paul supporters to include language opposing nation building overseas, foreign aid, and the NDAA.[59]

In the lead-up to the convention, Dr. Paul's Audit the Fed legislation passed the House of Representatives on July 25 by a large margin, 327-98, compared to years earlier when he could not muster the necessary support for it to be voted on.

There was no doubt that the Ron Paul grassroots support had taken ground in winning delegates at individual Republican state conventions throughout the country in 2012. It was a legitimate strategy, and it amassed a large number of delegates. However, the party establishment, helped by the corporate media, did everything it could to snatch away or change the rules after the fact. As reported by NPR and Fox News. com, Paul's Maine delegates' numbers were reduced at the convention by party rules. Bernie Johnson, a Maine Paul delegate, was quoted as saying, "There were people who were frustrated with the rule change, with the

---

[57]    Ibid.

[58]    Mark Preston, "Ron Paul delegates set to strike deal with RNC," CNN, http://politicalticker.blogs.cnn.com, August 21, 2012.

[59]    Kevin Kelly, "Ron Paul: The last Republican Challenger," Washington Times, http://communities.washingtontimes.com, September 4, 2012.

way people were treated." He also stated that he "never thought" it would be so hard to promote limited government and "peace."[60]

Ashley Ryan, a twenty-one-year-old college student, who is Maine's national committeewoman, was a Paul delegate at the national convention. Due to a credentials battle, GOP party leaders left Maine with half of its delegates that the Paul forces had won fairly at the state GOP convention. After many hours of discussion, the committee on credentials voted unanimously to replace ten Paul delegates with ten aligned with Romney. It was a "blunt reminder of Mitt Romney's grip on the national convention proceedings."[61] Ryan stated, "It was a huge slap in the face. I was very disappointed." Thanks to the Iowa delegation, unseated Maine delegates were able to use guest passes to attend the convention.

Former Maine state lawmaker Stavros Mendros said, "It's going to be a disaster back home. People are going to be out for blood."[62] But prior to the decision being finalized, twenty-three state of Maine GOP leaders, in a letter circulated in early August, demanded that top party figures allow Paul supporters to go to Tampa. The letter attacked Maine Republican National committeewoman Janet Martens Staples, who had filed a challenge to fourteen pro-Paul delegates and alternates. Those who joined together to issue the letter called Staples actions "destructive to party unity" and negative to the maintenance of majorities in the Maine Legislature, calling for her to resign.[63] Staples was a well-known Romney supporter and served on the party's executive committee. Ironically, when the contest to Paul's Maine delegates initially emerged, the Contest Committee made a finding "that there was not enough evidence to invalidate the state convention or to rule against the delegates." Instead of dismissing the whole issue at that point, the "RNC kicked it down the

---

[60]   Judson Berger, "Ron Paul supporters protest in halls of convention," http://politics.blogs.foxnews.com, August 29, 2012.

[61]   John Harwood, "Libertarian legion stands ready to accept torch from Paul," New York Times, http://www.nytimes.com, August 25, 2012.

[62]   Brian Bakst, "Ron Paul's aura leaves GOP, Romney in tricky spot," Associated Press, http://bigstory.ap.org/article, August 24, 2012.

[63]   "Paul delegate purge sparks GOP civil war in Maine," http://www.buzzfeed.com/buzzfeedpolitics/, August 2, 2012.

line for a few more weeks," maintaining they would resolve it finally in Tampa.[64]

In the lead-up to the convention in Tampa, "Hundreds of delegates for Paul were emerging and insider estimates were claiming that as many as 500 or more had been legally elected out of the caucus states and some primary states." But the media tried to tell a different story by either saying that Paul had far fewer delegates than his actual count or that those delegates would have to vote for Romney anyway. However, Rule 38 adopted by the national GOP from the prior 2008 national convention was in place, essentially allowing any delegate to vote their conscience on any ballot. Benn Swann of Fox 19 Cincinnati had emphasized this point in one of his "Reality Check" segments. It was the thinking of the Paul campaign strategists and the hope of many of the Paul delegates and other supporters among the electorate that if there were enough Paul delegates to prevent Romney from gaining the needed 1,144 delegates to obtain the nomination on the first ballot, a brokered convention might ensue, raising Paul's chances at the convention in Tampa.

However, at the convention itself and deciding against the wishes of the attendees, the GOP establishment decided to change the rules at the last minute to require that a potential presidential nominee must now have an eight state delegate plurality in order to be added to the first ballot. Furthermore, the GOP was changing the 2008 rule which stated that no delegate can be bound to vote for any one candidate in particular. They were changing it to essentially require that delegates would have to vote for the candidate that won their particular state and that RNC officials can remove or replace any delegates they choose for whatever reason they deem appropriate. It was these kinds of rule maneuverings that essentially were responsible for Paul's forces coming to Tampa with fewer than half of the delegates he could have had. Barring this kind of behavior given full dispensation and cover by a media that did not expose the depth of such deceptive practices, Paul's forces were reduced in number.

Paul's campaign manager, John Tate, in correspondence to supporters in August 2012, noted that while all the attempts to de-credential delegates were occurring at the convention, the Romney campaign

---

[64]  Tom Mullen, "The real story behind those Ron Paul delegates from Maine," Washington Times, http://communities.washingtontimes.com, September 2, 2012.

DEBORAH K. SMARTH

did not become involved, but "they've sat idly by on the sidelines." As he noted, "one would think the Romney campaign would want these conflicts resolved so they didn't become major issues at the Convention."

Ron Paul stopped campaigning actively in primary states that had not yet voted, but his campaign had not stopped. Toward the end of June 2012, despite the incredible number of delegates, Ron Paul won at many state GOP conventions, congressman and GOP presidential candidate Ron Paul conceded that he did not have quite enough delegates to take over the convention but wanted to ensure that his duly elected delegates were seated and had input into the Republican national platform. During his interview on MSNBC's *Morning Joe*, Paul indicated that if he was not going to be the nominee or give a speech on the floor of the convention, but he would like a meeting to say, "Look, we have numbers, we have people, we have enthusiasm, we believe in something. Why don't you pay a little attention?" He indicated, "I think they are (paying attention). They don't know quite how to handle it."

While his supporters pushed for a prime speaking slot for Dr. Paul at the national convention, inevitably, the party decided to present a very brief video highlighting Ron Paul's political career, highlighting how he took the less traveled path. His son, U.S. Senator Rand Paul from Kentucky, who had decided after the Paul presidential campaign acknowledged that they did not have enough delegates to the national convention to potentially win, announced he would support Mitt Romney. Senator Paul was granted a speaking slot in lieu of his father. Interestingly, it was reported in the weeks leading up to the convention that presidential candidate Ron Paul would have to submit his speech to the RNC and the Romney team for vetting and approval, and he would also have to fully endorse Mitt Romney for president. Knowing the independence of Ron Paul and the fact that there were large numbers of Ron Paul delegates and supporters going to Tampa, it was no surprise that he declined to push for such an address as he stated it would then not be his speech. As reported by the *New York Times*, Paul is quoted as saying that under those circumstances, "it wouldn't be my speech," and "that would undo everything I have done in the last 30 years. I don't fully endorse him (Romney) for President."

A Paul staff member told Policymic, a web-based news site, that "Ron Paul makes his own decisions, but based on past experience, he's not going to endorse Romney for three reasons; Romney's not principled,

Romney doesn't share Paul's views on almost any key issue, and Romney has little chance of winning."

Another staffer of Ron Paul commented, "Anything that could be seen as support for Romney's policies just wouldn't make much sense after a forty year career of not compromising for political expediency. It's very, very unlikely that Ron would issue a statement like the one Rand [his son] did."[65]

Poignantly stated in the *American Conservative*, "There is little congruence between the views of Romney and Paul. Romney is a plutocratic imperialist unlikely to diminish unconstitutional big government at home or abroad. Paul is the opposite." His following is grounded in Paul's principles. "Paul stands for something beyond a desire for personal power. His is a campaign of ideas. Romney seems to be one of those odd persons who has wanted to be president his entire life . . ."[66] It was reported that as all eyes were focused on McCain during the 2008 Convention, Romney quietly started his campaign by focusing on the Rules Committee, then in order to lay the groundwork for the 2012 nomination.

Prior to the large rally that would be organized by the Paul campaign for his supporters and delegates, Ron Paul told supporters in a video message on the Internet that it would be important to keep a positive demeanor and that "if the tone is positive, we're more likely to have success."[67] Paul always encouraged his supporters to be respectful.

Ron Paul's campaign organized a large event nearby to the Republican National Convention at the University of South Florida's Sun Dome, where Ron Paul gave his final address to a packed crowd (an estimated ten thousand plus) on August 26, prior to the RNC event. Billed as the "We are the Future Rally," Ron Paul's supporters in the Liberty movement gathered to hear their leader's important speech. Ron Paul had been quoted as saying that this was "the speech the RNC does not want

---

[65]  Natalie Littlefield, "Ron Paul stays mum on vote for Mitt Romney," The Capitol Column, http://www.capitolcolumn.com/news, July 22, 2012.

[66]  Jeff Taylor, "The GOP has a long tradition—shared by George Romney—of open disagreements at the convention," American Conservative, http://www.theamericanconservative.com, July 16, 2012.

[67]  Stewart Powell, "Ron Paul misses cut to address delegates at Tampa convention," Minneapolis Star Tribune, http://www.startribune.com/politics, July 16, 2012.

the rest of America to hear." While this newsworthy event did not receive the coverage it deserved by the American corporate media, the foreign press from around the world did take note just like many people in foreign countries took note of the candidacy of Dr. Paul throughout the presidential nomination process. Prior to the event according to campaign sources, "nearly 90 major media outlets" had already reserved spots at this important rally. At that rally, Paul was discussing foreign policy when he alluded to, "Somebody . . . said the other day on the Internet, 'if those Paul people had been in charge, Osama Bin Laden would still be alive.'" Paul countered with emotion: "But you know what I think the answer is? So would the 3,000 people [killed] on 9/11, be alive."[68] In response to that statement, the crowd enthusiastically applauded.

Many supporters of Paul across the nation had been truly disappointed in Senator Rand Paul (Kentucky) and the talk and blogged comments among some supporters and delegates alike suggested that Rand Paul, campaign chairman Jesse Benton, and official blogger for the Ron Paul campaign Jack Hunter were "more concerned with playing nice with the GOP establishment than in doing the right thing that Ron Paul has done during his entire career; stand up for the 'truth' and not compromise it." Many shared exchanges on the Internet site of the Daily Paul and other venues suggested that Ron Paul probably went along with Rand's decision as "to throw a small olive branch to the GOP party with the hope of influencing the party platform." When Ron Paul's son, Senator Rand Paul, decided to officially endorse Romney, his action "incurred the wrath of Ron Paul supporters."

Talking of the disappointed Ron Paul followers, Maine delegate and national committeewoman Ashley Ryan commented about Rand Paul's endorsement of Romney, "There were a lot of people who were upset. Rand's going to have a lot of work ahead of him to secure his base if he wants to be the next liberty candidate."

It was reported, though, "that as an olive branch to Ron Paul and his supporters, the Romney campaign asked his son, Senator Rand Paul, to speak in prime time at the opening of the Convention."[69]

---

[68] Erica Ritz, "Ron Paul: 9/11 victims would still be alive if 'Paul people had been in charge," http://www.theblaze.com, August 26, 2012.

[69] Mark Preston, "Ron Paul delegates set to strike deal with RNC," CNN, http://politicalticker.blogs.cnn.com, August 21, 2012.

When asked if the Republican Party had lost its way, Ron Paul indicated that on many issues of substance—no serious distinctions between the Republicans and Democratic parties exist. In comparing Presidents Barack Obama and George W. Bush, Paul maintained, "They're both very militaristic, interventionist, pro-war . . . Do Republicans really stop welfare expansion? No. Do they really cut back and balance the budget? No. They usually introduce bigger budgets." He further noted that in terms of the philosophy of government, there was not enough of a difference between the parties.

Paul viewed his candidacy as a way of influencing the convictions of the Republican Party. He noted that "there were times when they had much better positions. And there's no reason why we can't restore those and improve upon them."[70] Paul had also encouraged his followers to be "respectful and dignified" at the national convention. There were "all sorts of high-level talking going on between the Mitt Romney and Ron Paul camps to make sure the Texas Libertarian's troops don't disrupt the GOP convention."[71] While demonstrating their vociferous support for their candidate, they still maintained a dignified presence despite the poor treatment they received at the national convention.

When it became apparent that Paul did not have enough delegates to overcome Romney's delegate numbers, his supporters began planning and organizing a massive event on the eve of the Republican National Convention to celebrate their ideas. Yet many of Paul's delegates and supporters still held out hope of influencing the nomination outcome. In 2008, his campaign held an event which was sold out at the Target Center in Minneapolis while the Republicans held their convention. Paul had not been invited to the 2008 convention even though he had been a Republican presidential candidate. He made it a point, however, to show up briefly at the 2012 national convention to circulate among the state delegations which strongly supported his candidacy to thank them once again for all they had sacrificed and done to advance the cause of liberty.

Despite Paul's strides at influencing a strong grassroots following, championing limited government, and raising the consciousness of

---

[70]   Kevin Robillard and Tim Mak, Politico, "Ron Paul backers won't take over, but he hopes party will embrace them," Las Vegas Sun, http://www. lasvegassun.com/news, June 21, 2012.

[71]   Rick Dunham, "Minnesota delegation to GOP convention is sticking with Ron Paul," http://blog.chron.com/txpotomac/2012/08, August 22, 2012.

DEBORAH K. SMARTH

monetary policy of the Federal Reserve, "Republican leaders still view Paul as an oddity they prefer to keep at a distance. For the second time, they've denied him a speaking slot at the Republican National Convention . . . His loud, tireless adherents are fuming—and say they won't rest until they see their man on the podium in Tampa."[72] Paul addressed his supporters at the University of South Florida's Sun Dome immediately prior to the commencement of the national convention. The event was organized by his campaign.

The RNC had first pick on the venues in Tampa during the week of the convention. The organizer of the so-called Paul Festival, different from the actual Paul campaign rally at the Sun Dome, released a statement on June 1 that the RNC had blocked an attempt to secure the fairgrounds. Some believed that the Republican Party was apprehensive about such an event since the convention is supposed to be an info-commercial to unite the party around a nominee. Even after Romney secured a Texas primary win, NPR reported that Romney still did not have enough delegates bound to vote for him in the first ballot at the convention.[73] It was also reported that even though there was an undetermined number of delegates bound to him that are actually Paul supporters, there could be a possibility that if Romney failed to obtain the 1,144 votes on the first ballot, the Paul supporters would vote for Paul at the next chance. You can imagine that these sound bites added fuel for hope by those involved and participating in Paul's campaign journey.

Even the *New York Times* editorial page editor's blog entitled "The Ron Paul Revolt" noted that Ron Paul's supporters "did wage a small-scale revolt in Tampa." It cited the fact that Nevada delegates attempted to nominate Mr. Paul from the floor by submitting petitions along with Minnesota, Maine, Iowa, Oregon, Alaska and the Virgin Islands. "That should have done the trick: Rules require signatures from just five states. But the party changed the rules on the spot. Henceforth, delegates must

---

[72]   Elizabeth Dwoskin, "Short-timer Ron Paul's Last Shot at Legalizing Pot," Bloomberg Businessweek, http://www.businessweek.com/articles, July 20, 2012.

[73]   Tom Mullen, "Republican Party blocking massive Ron Paul event in Tampa?" Washington Times, http://communities.washingtontimes.com, June 2, 2012.

gather petitions from eight states."[74] In addition, during the official roll call to nominate former governor Romney, seventeen delegates from Nevada voted their conscience and supported Dr. Paul. This infuriated the former Republican governor of Nevada, Robert List.

A transcript from *Democracy Now* broadcast on NPR by host and executive producer Amy Goodman reported some important and truthful news when Nermeen Shaikh, reporting from the Republican National Convention floor, provided a news account that documented "a major eruption of fury" at the convention as the nomination process began when part of the Maine delegation "stormed off the floor in protest against a decision to strip away half of the state's Ron Paul delegates." Amy Goodman cited the fact that the RNC replaced ten of the twenty Paul delegates, "enough to prevent Ron Paul from being nominated from the floor."[75]

According to Ron Paul supporter and delegate Brad Linzy from Indiana, "Ron Paul supporters who have followed all the rules to become duly elected delegates to represent the other Republicans in the conventions have seen their delegate status challenged and many have been arbitrarily removed by high party officials in the name of presenting a 'united front' for the cameras. The Republican National Committee has violated its own rules on numerous occasions in this effort to quell dissent."[76]

For instance, the RNC effectively prevented a truly successful attempt by Paul supporters of entering Ron Paul's name into nomination at the convention in Tampa by changing the rules so that the threshold for placing a candidate's name in official nomination was increased from five to eight states. The RNC also arbitrarily removed ten duly elected Ron Paul delegates from the state of Maine's delegation and named supporters of Romney as delegates to prevent a motion being made by the state delegation that would advance Paul's nomination. When calls for a paper

---

[74] Juliet Lapidos, "The Ron Paul Revolt," New York Times, http://takingnote. blogs.nytimes.com, August 28, 2012.

[75] Transcript, "Chaos on the Convention Floor as RNC Blocks Ron Paul Delegates, Alters Seating Rules," Democracy Now, http://www. democracynow.org, August 29, 2012.

[76] Brad Linzy, "Snubbing Ron Paul, the RNC may have cost Romney the election," Huffington Post, http://www.huffingtonpost.com, August 31, 2012.

DEBORAH K. SMARTH

or roll-call ballot were requested, there are videos that exist with the chairman of the convention refusing to hear such requests to prevent any further action.

In addition, reports from Ron Paul delegates at the convention itself maintained that they were being forced to first sign an agreement conjured up by the Romney team "saying they will not oppose anything to collect their credentials to enter the convention." Other reports maintained that in those states where Paul had a majority of delegates, their transportation to the convention either were running late or were redirected. Republican longtime operative, Morton Blackwell from Virginia, who opposed the RNC's changing rules to dissuade or circumvent grassroots participation through the delegate process, maintained (in a video) that the transportation mode delays for certain states' delegations were probably unintended. Yet, as reported, "Many of Paul's supporters and other delegates were left stranded at various locations around the city while others were purposely driven around for hours in buses, unable to attend the convention for lengthy periods of time."[77]

A delegate from Virginia, Christopher Stearns, who happened to be a bus passenger, posted on his Facebook page on August 28, 2012, that "the Virginia and Rhode Island delegations are apparently being blocked from entering the Republican National Convention. They're keeping us all on a bus and not allowing us in the security perimeter."[78] Some had maintained that the Virginia delegation bus was being redirected away from the convention to prevent the Ron Paul delegates from voting against the Rules Committee power grab. In certain accounts, some maintained that rule changes occurred only "because Morton Blackwell and other astute Republican leaders were kept away from the convention by hijacked buses that circled for hours, with delegates screaming, 'Let us off this bus.'" According to RNC alternate delegate Josiah Tillet of Bedford, Virginia, the Iowa, Minnesota, and Rhode Island delegations were "delayed with similar transportation issues."[79]

---

[77] Jeffrey Phelps, "How the GOP stole the nomination," http://www. examiner.com, August 31, 2012.

[78] "Virginia delegation bus being directed away from convention...", Posted on http://www.dailypaul.com/251570, August 28, 2012.

[79] "Updated-Virginia RNC delegation prevented from voting on rule changes," http://virginia6th.teapartywatchdogs.com/2012, August 28, 2012.

The Paul campaign lawyer, in advance of decisions being made on delegates' unseating in certain states, approached the Republican National Committee's Committee on Contests, warning that "a political battle could erupt" over the refusal to seat Paul delegates. His representation of the Paul campaign, in light of the clear games that were being played by the party leadership, was met with resistance, of course. Convention vice chairman Solomon Yue told the *Washington Times* that the Paul attorney "turned a rules challenge into political blackmail" and "was thuggish."[80] Quite to the contrary, it certainly appeared that the actions of the national GOP showed true disregard for those Paul delegates who were newcomers to the party and who wanted to naturally promote and support their candidate.

During the week prior to the official commencement of the national convention, Paul's campaign was seeking to appeal the stripping of Paul delegates that won at the Louisiana state convention back in June 2012. The initial request in early August was rejected, but a subsequent attempt—with a formal letter sent to the RNC—was made the week prior to the kickoff of the national convention as reported by CNN. The Paul campaign maintained that the Louisiana GOP state executive committee replaced unallocated delegates at the state convention "after it sent out a memo to convention participants outlining supplemental rule changes." Mr. Charles Davis, a Louisiana Paul campaign chairman, said that Ron Paul supporters only received notice of such changes two days prior to the convention, but these rule changes concerning how Louisiana elected national delegates were "clear violations of the national requirement that all rules must have been submitted to the RNC last October 1[2011]."[81] The Paul campaign chairman Jesse Benton was also quoted as saying that "some of the Texas Congressman's supporters were kept from voting during the selection process." He further stated that "the Louisiana GOP insiders, realizing they were in the minority, grossly and

---

[80] "Ron Paul convention delegates deal cut," United Press International, http://www.upi.com, August 21, 2012.

[81] Brian Doherty, "Ron Paul delegate roundup: His Massachusetts people lose, his Louisiana fight goes to round two," *Reason Magazine*, http://reason.com/ 2012/08/20, August 20, 2012; Staff of the Capitol Column, "Ron Paul continues fight to secure Louisiana delegates," http://www.capitolcolumn.com/news/ron-paul-continues-fight-to-secure-louisiana-delegates/#ixzz242y2kgY2, August 19, 2012.

DEBORAH K. SMARTH

repeatedly violated their own party rules to try to railroad through their preferred delegation."[82]

In addition, it was reported on August 17 by the *Sun Journal* that several Maine delegates, including Stavros Mendros, Brent Tweed, and Matthew McDonald, filed a request for an injunction with the Belfast Superior Court in Maine to rule against the Republican National Committee's attempts to not seat twenty-one Paul delegates to the national convention. The GOP state chairman there had initially tried to make a deal by seating all contested Paul delegates and alternates in exchange for signed statements pledging to vote for presumptive nominee Mitt Romney if Mr. Paul's name did not appear on the ballot at the Tampa convention. Brent Tweed, the Maine delegation chairman, opposed the proposal by saying, "We will not be intimidated into signing political deals under threat of being unseated. We are accountable to the Maine Republicans who elected us, not the Mitt Romney campaign."[83]

Not only were Maine Paul delegates stripped of their delegate credentials, delegates from the states of Oklahoma, Louisiana, Nevada, and Massachusetts were unseated in favor of Romney delegates even though opposition from the floor arose. Points of order made by Paul delegates were downright ignored by the GOP powers to be. Recordings by individuals of the proceedings from the floor document that the presiders of the convention "purposely skipping over portions of the proceedings (teleprompter part 2) that would have allowed for a fair fight."[84] It was quite obvious that the system at work favored Romney as the party's nominee.

In a November 8, 2012, letter to supporters, former Paul campaign manager and current president of Campaign for Liberty, John Tate, said that after witnessing the occurrences on the floor of the Republican National Convention, railroading party rules developed "to weaken the power of grassroots activists of every stripe . . . The mood inside the

---

[82]  Adam Levy, "Ron Paul campaign to challenge all Louisiana delegates," CNN, http://politicaltickerblogs.cnn.com, July 27, 2012.

[83]  David Sherfinski, "Ron Paul backers fight effectively for GOP goals," Washington Times, http://www.washingtontimes.com/news, August 8, 2012.

[84]  Jeffrey Phelps, "How the GOP stole the nomination," http://www.examiner.com, August 31, 2012.

building at that moment was hard to describe. People were frustrated. They were confused and hurt. Many felt betrayed."

A month before the convention, a press release issued on July 27, 2012, reported that sixteen Massachusetts-elected Liberty Caucus delegates/alternates to the Republican National Convention who had been decertified by the Massachusetts Republican Party formally filed a challenge with the Republican National Committee. They were duly elected on April 28, defeating powerful establishment Republicans. The Massachusetts GOP Delegate Allocation Committee, the release says, "ignored all other evidence, and unanimously concluded that these 16 delegates would not honor Republican Party rules, and refused to certify them." The release says that these elected delegates pledged to follow Massachusetts law and Republican Party rules and had signed affidavits but were purged regardless.

These people, who came to Tampa, winning their delegate seats fairly and under the rules in place at their respective state GOP conventions, invested hours, days, weeks, months, and years campaigning for their candidate. They even spent their own personal monies to participate at these many party functions and events to help support their candidate's chances of winning only to lose their credentials by abruptly, enacted national party rule changes which disenfranchised them at the national convention.

According to vote tallies at the National Convention posted at www.ingotnews.com, Ron Paul had about two hundred delegates who cast their votes at the convention for him. On this site, it denotes that "there were countless other delegates who wanted to vote for Congressman Paul but were either forced to vote for Romney, coerced into it, or had their delegate positions illegally taken away from them" by the GOP establishment. The Internet site indicated that "there were plenty of shenanigans and rule-breaking by the establishment GOP but the Ron Paul folks still managed to make themselves be seen and heard."

At an August 27 delegation meeting, "of Colorado's 36 delegates, eight stopped short of supporting Romney and his running mate Representative Paul Ryan in a voice vote." As one twenty-three-year-old delegate, Jeremy Strand, indicated, "We hold our principles and our constitution higher than our party's success . . . All of us would agree that he (Romney) is not exactly a Republican."[85] Romney's credentials as a Conservative were challenged throughout the long campaign.

According to Josh Putnam, a campaign-elections expert who writes a political blog, "the Paul folks have flexed their muscle in 2012 and I imagine the RNC will punch back—not quell the rebellion, but figure out a way to incorporate these people that keeps them united as a party."[86] The actions taken at the national convention proved otherwise, though.

"The skirmishes with Paul supporters highlight lingering tensions between wings of the party ahead of a convention geared around unity. In a peace offering, Romney's campaign announced plans to air a video tribute to the Libertarian-leaning Paul during the convention." Senior Romney campaign aide added that the tribute "is a nod to Romney's respect for Paul." Russ Schriefer pointed out that while Romney and Paul had disagreed on many issues, "they always have had, if you've watched the debates this year, a lot of mutual respect between the two of them."[87] In addition, the Republican National Committee and the Ron Paul supporters had been negotiating over convention delegates that will be seated, and there was agreement on seating delegates from Massachusetts and Louisiana. A Paul official described the agreement as "a major step towards peace and good will on the convention floor."[88] But subsequently, deeds did not match these aspired hopes.

As NPR reported at the convention, "Romney and the RNC had been pursuing a legal strategy that appeared designed to prevent Paul from coming into the convention with the support of a plurality of the delegates from each of five or more states."[89]

Prior to the start of the Republican National Convention, the Rules Committee proposed and enacted rules that would blatantly prevent

[85]  Allison Sherry and Chuck Plunkett, "Some Colorado delegates hold out on Mitt Romney for Ron Paul," Denver Post, http://www.denverpost.com/nationalpolitics, August 27, 2012.

[86]  Liz Halloran, "Romney and GOP strike deal with Ron Paul loyalists before convention," NPR, http://m.npr.org/story/, August 22, 2012.

[87]  Brian Bakst, "Ron Paul's aura leaves GOP, Romney in tricky spot," Associated Press, http://bigstory.ap.org, August 24, 2012.

[88]  Mark Preston, "Ron Paul delegates set to strike deal with RNC," CNN, http://politicalticker.blogs.cnn.com, August 21, 2012.

[89]  Liz Halloran, "Romney and GOP strike deal with Ron Paul loyalists before convention," NPR, http://m.npr.org/story/, August 22, 2012.

Paul's name from being put into nomination. A Tennessee committee member, John Ryder, had initially wanted to raise the threshold of a plurality of delegates from the five states, which was in place during the various state GOP conventions in the lead-up to the national convention, to ten states. Morton Blackwell, a committee member from Virginia, opposed the measure, saying, "All we are talking about here—let's put it frankly—is the possibility that somebody like Ron Pau would be denied the possibility, after he carried five states, to have his name placed into nomination." Blackwell further commented that "this is a very bad idea. And we have got to, in this party, treat newcomers fairly. This would be taken as a slap in the face to grassroots people."[90] There were also attempts by the national committee to pass a rule that would have required that delegates at least one hour before they vote to provide their intention of who they will nominate. That rule was not passed. But as many of the Paul loyalists recognized, the fact that it was considered showed the concerns that the RNC and Romney campaign had concerning the voting intentions of Paul delegates.

As a Paul delegate from Nevada, Carl Bunce, said, "We want to redefine the party from the ground up. The natural step is to take it to the convention, though the establishment wants to mute any dissent for the imaginary 'party unity' that they produce as a giant TV show." Bunce added that "we're just asking for a fair, open and transparent process and Republicans have refused to give us that at a national level."[91]

"It is hard not to conclude that the entire war to unseat Paul's delegates was waged to silence him . . . Had all of Paul's delegates been seated . . . he would have been entitled to a 15 minute speech. Whether he would have persuaded a single Romney delegate is not important. What is important is that millions of television viewers would have heard that speech, a large percentage of whom have still probably never heard of Ron Paul . . . In short, a Ron Paul speech at the RNC would have been about really doing what Republicans claim they stand for but never actually do: Reduce the size and influence of the federal government. And it would have appealed not only to Republicans, but Democrats and Independents as well, just as Paul's campaign had during primary

---

[90]  Angel Clark, "RNC attempts to make Ron Paul ineligible for Republican nomination," http://www.examiner.com, August 23, 2012.

[91]  Liz Halloran, NPR, August 22, 2012.

DEBORAH K. SMARTH

season. This could not be allowed to happen. He could not be allowed to speak."[92]

Despite all the maneuvers, it was reported by the *Las Vegas Sun* that "Paul supporters led by Nevada delegate Wayne Terhune, succeeded in putting together petitions from six states to put Paul's name up for nomination." But as previously referenced, the Romney campaign won a critical rule change that raised the threshold from five states to eight. Despite that fact, "Paul supporters handed the petition to the Convention Secretary. Then, the Convention voted to adopt the eight-state rule, crushing the Paul effort."[93] The *New York Times* also reported that that "the party changed the rules on the spot."[94] The state delegates from Nevada, Minnesota, Maine, Iowa, Oregon, Alaska, and the Virgin Islands made such an effort. As Ms. Kathleen Gee blogged, "We managed, in spite of a corrupt media, corrupt national GOP, corrupt state GOP organizations, voter ignorance, voter apathy, a massive disinformation campaign, an ongoing psy-ops campaign, and physical violence, to get Ron Paul the GOP nomination, based on the rules of four days ago. The GOP and Democrat-controlled media had to lie, cheat, steal, and break bones to stop us."[95] Paul delegate Cindy Lake of Las Vegas further commented, "They said to us, you have no voice. Tea Party you have no voice. Liberty movement you have no voice."[96]

Perhaps the most endangering move that the Republican National Committee initiated was the passage of a rule which would essentially make it impossible to build up delegate support at statewide conventions as Paul had achieved during the 2012 nomination cycle. The rules would essentially prevent the latter practices and provide that the

[92] Thomas Mullen, "What Ron Paul didn't say," Washington Times, http://communities.washingtontimes.com, September 6, 2012.

[93] Anjeanette Damon, "Paul gets six petitions but falls short of having his name added to RNC ballot," Las Vegas Sun, http://www.lasvegassun.com/news, August 28, 2012.

[94] Juliet Lapidos, "The Ron Paul Revolt," New York Times, http://takingnote.blogs.nytimes.com, August 28, 2012.

[95] Posted comments by Kathleen Gee, http://www.dailypaul.com, August 29, 2012.

[96] Anjeanette Damon, "Paul gets six petitions but falls short of having his name added to RNC ballot," Las Vegas Sun, http://www.lasvegassun.com/news, August 28, 2012.

winner of actual state caucuses or primaries would inevitably win the allocated number of delegates to the national convention. Such a change would block real grassroots populism and promote the so-called party establishment's preferred candidate for nomination. According to one account, the first version of Romney proposed rules would have allowed the party's preferred nominee himself to choose all of the delegates in any state where the candidate won the primary. This rule would have totally gutted grassroots participation, rendering state conventions useless, and this attempt by the GOP leadership infuriated many Paul delegates as well as others at the convention.

On August 27, at a meeting of one hundred Texan delegates at the Saddlebrook Resort in Tampa, the rule changes fired up the entire state delegation. Delegate Melinda Fredricks publicly read a letter "condemning recent changes to the national Republican party's rules that would allow the GOP presidential candidate to veto and replace state delegates." She said, "Our delegates are in shock that such an amendment even would be presented before the Rules Committee much less passed into rule. Please know from the Texas delegation standpoint that the only way a floor fight can be avoided is for this rule to be stricken." She received resounding applause by a standing delegation. Besides the top Romney operatives, Governor Haley Barbour and other Romney supporters pushed for rules of this kind which were "intended to significantly weaken the power of grassroots politics and insurgent candidates such as Ron Paul." Many felt that such a rule change would help national candidates gain power to replace delegates, including the party faithful, with large donors and other friends.[97] It is interesting to note that while opposition to the rule changes began with Ron Paul supporters, further support grew within the entire Texas delegation and other significant parts of delegations from South Carolina, Colorado, Virginia, Louisiana, and elsewhere. Even, "Republican officials from Nevada called it a 'Marxist-style power grab.'" Sarah Palin, in her Facebook entry, labeled it "a direct attack on grassroots activists by the GOP establishment, and it must be rejected." Julianne Thompson, a Romney delegate and Georgia state Tea Party Patriots coordinator, said, "Our party is a grassroots party and not a top-down party."[98]

---

[97] Liz Goodwin, "Texas delegates planning floor mutiny over RNC rules changes," http://news.yahoo.com/blogs/ticket, August 27, 2012.

[98] Michele Goldberg, "Rules change sparks grassroots boos at GOP convention," Daily Beast, http://www.thedailybeast.com/articles, August 29, 2012.

Ben Ginsberg, Romney's top attorney, had engineered many of the rule changes, and John Sununu, another envoy of Romney, also helped direct proceedings at the Tampa Convention. In addition, further rule changes would empower the Republican National Committee to amend party rules without a full convention vote.[99] It was felt that the national GOP "began using this power in Tampa to purge the floor of Ron Paul delegates." A large problem existed, however. "Almost all of the Hispanics, African Americans and gays on the floor were Ron Paul supporters." Some media outlets as well as the *National Review* reported that the rule changes were an effort by Romney's lawyers to prevent a Conservative challenge to him in 2016.

Even national Conservative figure, Morton Blackwell, weighed in saying, "that the compromise the Party leaders are talking about is a fake that is meant to get Conservatives to back down and not to submit a minority report opposing these bad rule changes." In addition, other rules would allow the party to change rules between conventions with no approval from the delegates. [100]

Those in charge of the convention even went as far as seating other Paul state delegations in bleachers "where they could more easily be ignored." As the Houston Chronicle noted, the delegates from the Virgin Islands, Puerto Rico, American Samoa and the Northern Mariana Islands got better seats than Ron Paul supporters and delegates.[101]

On August 30, it was reported by eyewitnesses on the floor of the convention and cited in a newspaper account from the *Washington Examiner* that "RNC Chairman Reince Preibus and House Speaker John Boehner (on August 28) railroaded the party's grassroots in order to shut down any debate over rule changes or the decision to unseat 10 Paul delegates elected in Maine." On a YouTube video, convention participants were yelling, "Seat them now!" In addition, the video also shows that

[99]   Sean Sullivan, "Why Ron Paul's presidential campaign may be the last of its kind," Washington Post, http://www.washingtonpost.com/blogs/the-fix/wp/2012/08/24, August 24, 2012.

[100]  "Morton Blackwell: Fake GOP convention compromise. Conservatives must not back down! Demand roll call vote," http://www.dailypaul.com, August 30, 2012, and http://youtu.be/GfxpCu5qxx4, Interview of Ben Swann on the Jerry Doyle Show.

[101]  Kevin Kelly. "Ron Paul: The last Republican challenger," Washington Times, http://communities.washingtontimes.com, September 4, 2012.

party leaders on the convention floor simply ignored points of order and objections that were made very loudly. An actual video of the proceedings indicated "that the teleprompter at the two-minute mark read the 'ayes' have it and the chairs just read their scripts." Priebus and Boehner seemingly ignored the fact—as reported by those on the floor—that the nos "pretty clearly shouted louder." Yet the chair says, "The ayes have it."[102] Timothy Carney, who was on the floor at the time that these party leaders simply ignored calls for points of order and objections, said, "It's hard to get more undemocratic than simply making up the results of a floor vote."[103]

Another example of how poorly the Paul people were treated concerned a microphone being abruptly cut off when the Georgia delegation attempted to read the number of delegates accumulated by Ron Paul on the convention floor. [104] Rather than taking appropriate and proper vote tallies and listening to objections, the RNC leaders did not allow Ron Paul's name and delegate vote totals to be mentioned officially on stage, even when he won specific states. While the chair of individual state delegations would give tallies citing publicly Ron Paul's delegate numbers, the presiding officer at the convention podium only read off Romney delegate numbers.[105] It was reported by IngotNews.com that presidential candidate Ron Paul had delegate votes in twenty-six states.

In an August 29 interview with Ron Paul's son, Senator Rand Paul, CNN's Wolf Blitzer, even noted at the national convention that "Republican officials clearly snubbed Ron Paul." He had referred to the practice of the GOP leadership not citing the vote tallies from each of the states' delegations, whose chairs would publicly cite the breakout of delegates in their respective delegations, including Ron Paul's delegate numbers.

In an August 30, 2012, interview on *The Daily Show*, even former Republican National Committee (RNC) chairman, Michael Steele,

[102] "Republicans' 2012 teleprompter convention part 2," http://youtu.be/77W5OKStO5s, and "RNC Sham 2012," http://youtu.be/B39W91O-rUg, August 29, 2012.

[103] Timothy P. Carney, "Can Teleprompters Count Votes?", Washington Examiner, http://www.washingtonexaminer.com, August 30, 2012.

[104] Kevin Kelly, "Ron Paul: The last Republican challenger," Washington Times, http://communities.washingtontimes.com, September 4, 2012.

[105] "RNC Sham 2012," http://youtu.be/B39W91O-rUg, August 29, 2012.

acknowledged that the treatment that Ron Paul and his supporters received at the August 2012 convention was unbelievable. He said that "what the Republican National Committee did to Ron Paul was the height of rudeness and stupidity for this reason: Why would you alienate an individual who has the ability to attract a new generation of voters, who are already skeptical of your institution but are willing to at least listen through the vehicle of this individual and the words that he is saying? Why would you alienate them, get on the floor and not let them speak? Not have his name go up on the board and see the number of electoral votes that he receives? This is crazy!" In answer to the question posed to Steele, "Why would the GOP do this," Steele remarked, "They are afraid of that which they cannot control."[106]

Robin Koerner blogged, "In all fields of human endeavor, winning by cheating is losing. In a competition, when someone cheats, he gets disqualified. The disqualification does not make the runner-up the winner. Rather, it reveals that the man who appeared to be the runner-up had in fact been the winner all along. In the race for the GOP nomination for President, therefore, Ron Paul won."[107] These comments apparently seemed to capture the frustration of what had occurred prior to and during the actual nominating convention. On August 28, concerning the de-credentialing of delegates, Bryan Daughtry, a Maine delegate himself, who was speaking to Dana Bash of CNN, stated, "We would like to amend the credentialing report when it's brought to the floor and if that's possible, we would like to get our duly-elected delegates sat back on the floor. As far as my own personal resolve, if they're not willing to sit 7 out of 8 who are veterans, a priest, a pastor, a Native American, and countless women back on this floor, and allow the RNC nine-state committee who picked these other delegates to continue to sit here, I really don't want to participate after that. I will walk off the floor, yes."[108]

After engaging with his delegates on the floor of the convention to thank them, Ron Paul exited town. Lew Rockwell, a noted economist and chief executive officer of the Ludwig von Mises Institute as well as

---

[106] Excerpt of Interview with Michael Steele, "The Daily Show," http://youtu.be/2MPcTWCoBTM, August 31, 2012.

[107] Robin Koerner, The Blog, "Ron Paul won," Huffington Post, http://www.huffingtonpost.com, August 29, 2012.

[108] "Ron Paul delegate speaks out against GOP corruption on CNN," http://youtu.be/6G5bdjiAaGE, August 28, 2012.

Paul's longtime collaborator, reported that "Ron, Carol, and one of their granddaughters left the GOP snake pit . . . At the airport in Clearwater, eight TSA agents descended on them and ordered them not to board their private plane." They were seeking to screen the pilots, passengers, and their airplane in detail saying they would have to check the plane for explosives. Dr. Paul's wife, who had a pacemaker, refused to be screened. Paul's aide started to video "the whole rotten process," and the TSA then backed down and allowed them to go through.[109]

As associate professor of political studies, Jeff Taylor of Dordt College noted, "Allowing Ron Paul to be placed in nomination, allowing an old-fashioned demonstration to occur on the convention floor, and allowing unbound delegates to pay tribute to their champion by casting votes without pressure or hostility would be a wise move by Romney. Far from being an embarrassment or a sign of divisiveness, it would denote strength of personal character and political position. This would pre-empt 'convention chaos' and let the Paul campaign be more persuasive in its attempt to keep its delegates respectful and on-task."[110] Evidently, the Romney campaign and the Republican National Committee realized the strength of the Paul revolution and the Paul delegates' commitment and zeal for their candidate's principles and platform, which might have caught fire if allowed to happen on the floor at the convention in Tampa. So instead of graciously allowing the nomination rules and allowing votes of Paul delegates to be acknowledged on the convention podium, they disallowed any openness and transparency.

The Republicans seemed most nervous about Paul's adherence to a less militaristic approach and his opposition to wars of aggression. Why? That position has been at the root of the Republican tradition. As Associate Professor Jeff Taylor indicates, examples of that tradition included presidents such as Robert Taft, who advocated less empire building; Dwight Eisenhower, who warned against the military-industrial complex; and presidential candidate Barry Goldwater's leanings toward commonsense nationalism. Ronald Reagan, years earlier, was even quoted as saying, "Ron Paul is one of the outstanding leaders fighting for a

---

[109]  Yvonne Kelly, "Ron left Tampa yesterday," http://www.dailypaul.com (from www.lewrockwell.com), August 29, 2012.

[110]  Jeff Taylor, "The GOP has a long tradition . . . of open disagreement at the convention," American Conservative, http://www.theamericanconservative.com, July 16, 2012.

stronger national defense. As a former Air Force officer, he knows well the needs of our armed forces, and he always puts them first. We need to keep him fighting for our country."

Over the years, the two parties' national conventions have become less exciting and more scripted. These conventions do not allow dissent; there is no contest or debates. For the most part, these conventions are choreographed and provide for the respective parties' coronation of their respective nominees. The 2012 Republican national convention in Tampa was nothing more than the coronation of Mitt Romney as its nominee.

Paul campaign advisor, Doug Wead, blogged, "Mitt Romney's mean spirited National Convention, run by a team who has refined exclusion and pettiness to an art, will now rely more than ever on the socialism and failed economy of Barack Obama to get their man elected. The door of their campaign is shut for anyone else to come in. At the RNC there was no generosity in victory, no forgiveness, no open arms, no calls for unity. Only scowls. It is payback time. To an unlikely combination of evangelicals, homosexuals and other targeted groups, the pain of the Romney's will soon be unleashed upon them."[111]

It was clear that Ron Paul waged an effective campaign during which his presidential election committee raised $40.9 million dollars from regular folks, not corporate entities or other elitists. The campaign spent $38.9 million with a $2 million surplus.

Unfortunately, most Americans hadn't even realized the developments behind the scenes in the lead-up to the Tampa convention and the maneuverings and deceptive practices at the national convention itself. A candidate named Ron Paul, who inspired so many, including America's youth, who had won so many delegates to the national convention despite all odds, would not become the nominee to challenge President Obama. The actions taken by the Republican National Committee at its national convention would have lasting repercussions in the days and weeks ahead, leading up to Election Day.

---

[111]  http://dougwead.wordpress.com/2012/08/31/romneys-revenge.

# CHAPTER THREE

# Media Blackout: Marginalization of a Presidential Candidate of Great Integrity, Vision, and a Champion of Liberty

THE TREND IN media ownership has become much more concentrated and less diversified. A 2012 Fortune 500 list indicates that the mass media has now been reduced to five or six major corporations. These media conglomerates present their opinion makers and the so-called news of the day from their vantage points and attitudinal perspectives, oftentimes impacting on the type of coverage given to serious issues in politics and culture.

The media holds much power as it helps set the agenda. Television news accounts influence Americans. News reports provide criteria by which the public evaluates or looks at a candidate and incorporates what they know about the candidate, impacting on their judgments about that candidate. Thus, the manner in which the news media frames political, campaign issues, and the candidates' positions influences the way the public evaluates those political issues or candidates.

Since most Americans are busy and lack the time and possible interest in being informed on all political issues or elections, oftentimes, they rely on others to provide information which inevitably provides guiding posts as to their political views or stances. Thus, the news opinion makers, including so-called journalists and talk-show hosts, help shape public opinion.

This is why journalism needs to uphold the highest standards for reporting. The "Journalist Creed," as put forth by Walter Williams when he found the Missouri School of Journalism more than a century ago, states "that Journalists must be public trustees with the full measure of responsibility to the public. That accuracy and fairness are fundamental to good journalism. That a single standard of truth must prevail for all . . . and that suppression of the news is indefensible."

It was clear that the Founding Fathers saw that a representative democracy or republic could only exist with a free press. In the twenty-first century, a free press is the farthest from the truth and presents our political system with major challenges in terms of having an informed electorate to essentially cast votes on the basis of as much truthful information as possible. The Internet is another alternative in seeking out information from all sides, but it requires time and the will to research the issues at hand. Yet if one didn't follow Dr. Ron Paul via the Internet, blogs, and alternative and independent media, the rank-and-file voters would hardly know his positions, background, mission, and the army of grassroots people who supported him for the presidential Republican nomination.

It was noted that Paul had consistently polled in double digits and was running a statistical dead heat against President Obama in nearly every poll conducted after strong finishes in Iowa, New Hampshire, and South Carolina.[112] During the 2011-12 presidential campaign and in the lead-up to the GOP nomination, even though Dr. Paul was the last standing Republican candidate to Romney, the media either failed to report or significantly reduced coverage of this candidate. When the media did report, it was either done in a negative manner or there were inaccurate characterizations of his candidacy, his positions, and his strong delegate wins at Republican state conventions throughout the country. Some exceptions may have existed but not enough, indeed.

"Ron Paul's 2012 campaign, just like his 2008 one, was ignored since day one by the mainstream media and the punditry, which seemed ready from the beginning to bestow the nomination on former Massachusetts governor Mitt Romney."[113] It has been noted that Congressman Paul,

---

[112] Kristopher Denby, "Support for Ron Paul growing despite scant media coverage," http://www.examiner.com, January 31, 2012.

[113] Connor Adams Sheets, "Ron Paul 2012 Delegate Strategy Makes New Gains in Massachusetts, Alaska," International Business Times, http://www.ibtimes.com, April 30, 2012.

also a medical doctor, "has been couched by the mainstream media as an underdog, a sideshow candidate incapable of beating his establishment opponents and unworthy of much attention."[114] Yet he proved to be a strong and formidable force in certain primaries and caucuses in which he competed as well as at state conventions all the way to Tampa.

Steve Kornacki Jr., a political writer for Salon.com, was quoted as saying, "The experience of 2008 demonstrated that it's very easy to exaggerate the breadth of Paul's support and that his views (particularly on foreign policy) are so far outside the GOP mainstream that the party establishment will go to great lengths to make sure it doesn't expand beyond his base. That still seems to be the case today." What about comments by Eric Zorn of the *Chicago Tribune*? Zorn said, "In short, no, he will never be president of the United States and no, he is not a plausible contender for the GOP nomination, so those who are covering the campaign don't feel obliged to pretend otherwise." [115] There are so many examples of this tendency to downplay Paul's candidacy on the part of the national media throughout his presidential bid through Tampa. Certainly, these types of attitudes and other countless opinionated characterizations, both electronically broadcast and in print media, are evidence that we don't have a free press, and they certainly do not live up to the standards of true journalism.

Prior to the 2012 primary and caucus season, media pundits and political analysts declared that Ron Paul's support hovered about a 5 or 6 percent ceiling. Even following Paul's coming in second—fewer than two hundred votes of Congresswoman Michele Bachman in the August 2011 Iowa presidential straw poll, "nearly all of the major television media outlets (including CNN, NBC, CBS, and FOX) reported that a new 'top tier' of candidates had appeared, referencing Bachman, Mitt Romney, and Texas Governor Rick Perry." But Paul's close win actually seemed to go unnoticed.

Even host Jon Stewart on *The Daily Show* commented following the Iowa straw poll in which Paul came in a close second, "This

---

[114] Connor Adams Sheets, "Ron Paul 2012: Can he beat Romney now that Newt Gingrich is bowing out?", International Business Times, http://www.ibtimes.com, April 25, 2012.

[115] Thomas J. Lucente Jr., "Media blackout of Ron Paul is irresponsible journalism," http://lucente.org/wp/2011/08/21/column-media-blackout-of-ron-paul-is-irresponsible-journalism/#/axzz2Sv0LQhRQ, August 21, 2011.

pretending Ron Paul doesn't exist for some reason has been going on for weeks," in a segment aired August 2011 that skewered coverage of the libertarian-leaning Republican candidate.

Paul's spokesman, Jesse Benton, commented to the congressional newspaper *The Hill* (August 15, 2011) that "it is a travesty that Dr. Paul was ignored after his near statistical tie and historic vote total." Throughout the campaign as noted by Benton, Americans across the country have been demanding that the media cover Dr. Paul.[116]

*Politico*'s Roger Simon wrote in August 2011, "Ron Paul just got shafted. Why didn't Paul get the same credit for his organizational abilities as Bachmann did?"[117] Paul had garnered 4,671 votes, 152 votes less than Bachmann, but a strong second. Yet, as Simon indicates, candidate Bachmann appeared on several Sunday news show programs, but Paul "appeared on none." There were only a few news stories about Paul's strong showing "but, to most of the media he [Paul] remained an exotic, unworthy of attention," noted *Politico*'s Roger Simon.

In mid-August 2011, following Paul's close second place in the Iowa straw poll, Fox News interviewed Liz Trotta, author and Fox News contributor, and Katherine Mangu-Ward, a senior editor at *Reason Magazine*, concerning the subject of Ron Paul's lack of media coverage. Trotta is quoted as saying that despite Paul's strong showing in the Iowa straw poll coming in second, she noted that Paul "can't even get on a Sunday talk show." She also alluded to how the media seemed to ignore the straw poll and how they continually single out Romney. Mangu-Ward actually commented during the interview that Paul is "someone who is never going to be President; he knows that, the press knows that, everyone is behaving as he's never going to be President."[118] Paul supporters were not only disappointed but also outraged by the comments made by Mangu-Ward of *Reason magazine*.

Paul even acknowledged that although his candidacy was doing well and in the top tier compared to the other Republican candidates that

---

[116] Joe Pompeo, "Is the news media treating Ron Paul's presidential campaign unfairly?", http://www.news.yahoo.com/blogs/cutline, August 16, 2011.

[117] Roger Simon, "Ron Paul remains media poison," http://www.politico.com, August 15, 2011.

[118] Interview with Liz Trotta and Katherine Mangu-Ward on Fox News, "Ron Paul's lack of media coverage," http://www.youtube.com/watch?v=xn_vN_uf310 (uploaded on August 16, 2011).

there is a tendency on the part of the media not to cover his candidacy because his views are challenging the status quo and "so they just as soon not give us the coverage the others are getting and they will concentrate on establishment-type politicians." As reported by *Politico*, Ron Paul had only one full-time embedded reporter from NBC news on his campaign trail as of mid-March 2012. "For most political reporters, he is all but irrelevant to the future of the GOP contest."[119]

Why did the mainstream media block out truthful coverage of a February 20, 2012, Veterans March to the White House, popularly known as "Ron Paul is the Choice of the Troops," in support of Ron Paul's military and foreign policy positions? The media typically covers veterans' activities and should have done so concerning the veterans support and their statements made about America's Republican presidential candidate Ron Paul. However, the veterans march was not aired on cable or television. At least five hundred veterans and reservists from the Iraq and Afghanistan conflicts marched to the White House, chanting "President Paul" and turning their backs on the White House to symbolically protest the war, U.S. foreign policy, and overseas engagements of the Obama administration. The march was organized by Adam Kokesh, a veteran himself, who founded Veterans for Ron Paul. Interestingly, ABC reported about the demonstration on their blog; however, the network reported that only a few dozen veterans showed. ABC had to apologize and retract the report as there were five-hundred-plus veterans marching.[120] One Internet news account cited that one thousand veterans had marched.

What about when Reserve Corporal Jesse Thorsen was invited on stage by presidential candidate Ron Paul to address Paul's cheering supporters during a January 2012 Iowa rally? Thorsen, a ten-year veteran, was cut short in a CNN interview on January 3. He had served two tours in Afghanistan and was headed back for a third. On stage, Thorsen said, "If there's any man out there that's had a vision, it's definitely Ron Paul. His foreign policy is by far, hands down better than any other candidates out there, and I'm sure you all know that. We don't need to be picking fights overseas and I think everybody knows that, too." Soon thereafter, Thorsen received a reprimand from the army. But he said on a Veterans for Ron

---

[119]   Dylan Byers, "NBC pulls Ron Paul's last embed," Politico, http://www.politico.com, March 14, 2012.

[120]   "Ron Paul is the choice of the troops march on the white house (livestream)," http://www.ronpaul.com, February 20, 2012.

Paul online radio show, "Why can't a combat veteran go up on stage and support a presidential candidate in his best suit, which is his American uniform?" He also commented that the reprimand was "absolutely worth it" because "it gave me the platform to spread the message of liberty and constitutional freedom to more people." Further commenting about the reprimand, he said, "You've been a real bad soldier, don't do that again . . . Okay, I won't." As raised in an Internet news piece, "One has to question whether the same punishment would have been handed out if he had been seen endorsing anyone other than Ron Paul."[121] Thorsen had also given a speech at the veterans march to the White House in late February 2012. An e-mail message leaked prior to that march "by multiple active duty personnel revealed that the military issued a warning to troops encouraging them not to take part" in the event.[122]

Throughout the long trail and uphill challenges to the national GOP convention, the media did not live up to its journalistic responsibilities. "The lack of coverage does suggest a conventional wisdom among many journalists that he (Paul) can't win the Republican nomination," said Mark Jurkowitz of the Pew Project for Excellence in Journalism.[123]

According to the Pew Research study, Project for Excellence in Journalism, Ron Paul only received 24 percent campaign coverage in 2011 compared to other contenders or potential contenders like Mitt Romney, Newt Gingrich, Michele Bachmann, non-candidate Sarah Palin, non-candidate Donald Trump, Tim Pawlenty, Jon Huntsman, Rick Perry, Rick Santorum, and Herman Cain. Following his runner-up finish to Michele Bachmann in the August 2011 Iowa straw poll, Paul actually complained about lack of media coverage, accusing the press of "being frightened by me challenging the status quo and the establishment."

During the period January 1 through August 14, 2011, Paul was a "dominant newsmaker" in only 27 stories; "dominant" meaning featured in at least 50 percent of a story. This is strikingly different from the "dominant newsmaker" coverage for Romney in 120 stories. The Pew study ranked Ron Paul tenth in media coverage, even far behind

---

[121]  Steve Watson, "Army official reprimands soldier who spoke at Ron Paul rally," http://www.infowars.com, March 30, 2012.

[122]  Ibid.

[123]  Michael Ono, "Pew Study: Mainstream Media views Ron Paul a secondary character in 2012 election narrative," http://abcnews.go.com/blogs/politics, August 18, 2011.

non-candidates like Trump and Palin as well as floundering candidates like Newt Gingrich. Yet Paul was the only presidential candidate talking about real, substantive issues with rational solutions that mattered during the presidential campaign.

In an effort to assess the post Iowa straw poll coverage regarding candidates' television coverage, the Pew Research Center analysis also studied coverage on the three-network Sunday morning shows on August 14, the morning and evening network news programs on August 15, and four hours of prime-time cable and one hour of daytime from each of the three major cable news networks on August 15. That analysis documented that Paul was mentioned just 29 times compared with 371 times for Rick Perry, 274 times for Michele Bachmann, and 183 times for Mitt Romney.

While some have argued that Paul had, in some instances, more appearances on cable television and Sunday news programs than the other candidates in 2011 since announcing his candidacy in May of that year, one can also argue that Paul was simply more available to the press because he is not an establishment candidate and took every opportunity to get out his message whenever press requests arose. Before Herman Cain's exit due to accusations of sexual harassment, Cain had more individual face time with news anchors than Paul, leading to Cain's temporary spike in the polls.[124] Yet it has been pointed out that even though Paul had outpaced other Republican candidates in national and state polls, "Paul is mentioned on air far less frequently than most of his rivals." The Project for Excellence in Journalism (PEJ) study noted that "for much of 2012, the tone of Paul's coverage was more positive than negative. But the glaring lack of attention in the news coverage reflected a media consensus that despite a loyal following and some respectable primary showings, the libertarian-leaning candidate could not capture the Republican nomination."[125] The media's pronouncements of "unelectable" in many instances influenced the electorate's perception of candidate Ron Paul.

The Pew Research Center's Project for Excellence in Journalism (PEJ), studying how the media covered the 2012 primary presidential campaign,

---

[124] Sarah Mimms, "Ron Paul ignored by the media? Not so much," National Journal, http://www.nationaljournal.com, December 22, 2011.

[125] Tom Rosenstiel, Mark Jurkowitz, and Tricia Sartor, "How the media covered the 2012 primary campaign," Pew Research Center (PEJ), http://www. journalism.org/anlaysis_report/RonPaul, April 23, 2012.

had other findings which indicated that while Paul received a more consistently positive portrayal of any candidate in the presidential race, the coverage "was offset by the fact that the media virtually ignored him." During the period January 2 through April 15, 2012, the study contends that "Paul was a significant figure in only seven percent of the campaign stories." "He received about one-eighth as much coverage as Romney and about one-quarter as much as Santorum and Gingrich." The study pointed out that only in the first two weeks of 2012 did Paul "register in more than 10 percent of the campaign stories," when he had solid showings in both Iowa and New Hampshire. "Paul's narrative turned negative for the first time the week of March 19-25. And it never returned to positive territory as the coverage began focusing on his increasingly quixotic effort." [126] The media's coverage influenced voter perceptions. Unless one was closely following the Paul campaign and his positions, many voters seemed to have fallen prey to the dismissive and oftentimes fallacious characterizations of Paul's candidacy by the press.

The analysis also noted that only "three percent of Paul's coverage scrutinized his personal background or public record, the lowest of any candidate in the primaries."[127] The study acknowledges that lesser scrutiny was most likely related to the fact that the media consensus maintained "that Paul could not win and thus, no extensive look, at his history and biography was warranted."

It is also interesting to note on what issues the media coverage focused in this presidential campaign during the Republican primary lead-up to the national convention. According to the Pew research study covering the period of November 1, 2011, through April 15, 2012, 64 percent of the coverage examined issues relating to polls, advertising, fundraising, strategy, and the continual question of who is winning and who is losing. Twelve percent of the coverage focused on personal issues like the candidates' personal backgrounds (families, religion, finances, etc.). In stark contrast, only 9 percent of the coverage related to national domestic issues and 1 percent on foreign policy issues. The fact that domestic and foreign policy issues received the lowest coverage is amazing, considering that the national economy was weak and our involvement in wars and overseas engagements are bleeding the American

---

[126] Rosenstiel, Jurkowitz, and Sartor, "How the media covered the 2012 primary campaign."

[127] Ibid.

taxpayers of their country's wealth. Yet on these two very important policy categories, presidential candidate Ron Paul had the strongest spending cut plan to deal with the national debt and deficit, had the strongest plank for eliminating taxation on the American people to keep more of their hard-earned dollars, had the strongest plan to eradicate wasteful Pentagon spending and wanted to end the wars, making it a last resort. These positions should have been his strongest attributes in a campaign waged with little differences among the other contenders for the Republican nomination and inevitably with the incumbent president of the Democratic Party. Incredibly, several months after the national presidential election, the very issues on which Paul continually focused—which did not receive the full coverage it deserved during the campaign—are now mentioned by political pundits and corporate media reporters and commentators without even the slightest reference to Paul.

All you had to do is view the GOP presidential debates and see the bias in how they treated presidential candidate Ron Paul. From limiting the number of questions in debates asked of Dr. Paul in contrast to the field of other contenders to the types of questions and demeanor in which they posed them. It was evident that "Paul gets less time to air his views in debates." Eric Ostermeier, political science professor from University of Minnesota, calculated that "Paul has had the least amount of time to speak in three of the last 10 debates; only twice has he been given more time than the average candidate."[128]

In fact, due to a large volume of complaints following the South Carolina debate that the post-debate analysis had excluded Ron Paul's showings by viewers on the charts and graphs presented by Fox News reporter John Roberts, Fox Anchor Harris Falkner commented, "John, you caused a fury in my world . . . I have a bone to pick with you. You left off Ron Paul." Twitter survey results eliminated Paul's name, entirely, "concerning which candidate most accurately answered questions and who had performed best." Yet it was clear that he had scored higher than any other candidates in the debate.

"The fact that Ron Paul was the outright winner of the debate was remarkable, given the fact that the moderators had done their utmost to exclude, smear and misrepresent the Congressman earlier in the

---

[128] Sarah Mimms, "Ron Paul ignored by media? Not so much," National Journal, http://www.nationaljournal.com, December 21, 2011.

DEBORAH K. SMARTH

night."[129] During that particular debate, "with almost every question the Congressman had to begin his answer by correcting the moderators for grossly distorting his position on multiple issues." Those issues included the difference between "defense spending" and Pentagon waste and Paul defending himself against Fox Moderator Bret Baier who "essentially called Paul a terrorist sympathizer" to which Paul retorted by explaining that he voted to go after Bin Laden following 9/11 and had introduced legislation to focus on the target rather than becoming embroiled in wars and nation building.

During the South Carolina GOP debate, the crowd actually took note and started demanding that Paul be given the opportunity to participate fully like the other contenders, forcing the CNN debate host to allow Paul to answer the same question the other three candidates were allowed to answer. "Excluding and ignoring Paul was, and has been a common theme throughout both the 2008 and the 2012 GOP nomination races, during every single debate since the very beginning."[130] In a debate moderated by John King, King of CNN "ignored Ron Paul twice, on two issues very much related to his years spent being a doctor. The issue of media blackout has become so obvious that politician comedian Jon Stewart devoted a segment of his show to that issue in August." "The media has treated Ron Paul as either invisible or insignificant."[131] This treatment of Paul's candidacy applied to both liberal and conservative media oftentimes.

It was apparent that the treatment presidential candidate Ron Paul received in the media, including C-Span's reduced coverage of Paul's speeches as the campaign moved onward in 2012 as compared with the other presidential contenders, was markedly different. In December 2011, CNN news journalist Gloria Borger hammered Paul until after trying his best to answer her questions, he finally shut off his microphone and politely departed. "This was a total hit job, bringing up decades old accusations about a newsletter that everyone agrees was written by others,

---

129 Steve Watson, "Media Manipulation Video: Fox News caught completely excluding Ron Paul from post-debate coverage-January 18, 2012," http://www.Prisonplanet.com, January 17, 2012.

130 Jeffrey Phelps, "Iowa vote fraud official," http://www.examiner.com, January 21, 2012.

131 Joseph Coleman, Yahoo Contributor Network, "Ron Paul: The invisible candidate?", Yahoo Voices, http://voices.yahoo.com, January 27, 2012.

while Dr. Paul was practicing medicine . . . most of the charges were made by people who couldn't have read the newsletters in full context."[132] Paul clearly stated that he did not read the article at the time of publication, did not write it, and disavowed it. Interestingly, Gloria Borger is married to a chief communications strategist for a company in Washington, D.C., which contracts with parts of the military industrial complex including the U.S. Army. One of Dr. Paul's major proposed policies was to reduce the strength of the military industrial complex.

Despite Paul's good, strong showing in Iowa, trailing Romney by only 3,769 votes, his second place showing in the New Hampshire primary, beating Gingrich by a two to one margin, the media (liberal or conservative) failed to tell the story. In New Hampshire, where Jon Huntsman took third place and ended up dropping out of the campaign afterward, he "actually received 13 percent of media coverage to Paul's 14 percent" even though Paul placed stronger and ended up being the last remaining challenger to Mitt Romney many months later.[133]

When Paul's campaign decided to issue a statement saying that they would not be competing in certain states that have yet to hold primaries because of a much more targeted strategy due to constrained campaign resources, the media erroneously reported that Ron Paul had dropped out of the presidential race entirely. And instead of correcting their reporting inaccuracy, the information was repeated oftentimes, further confusing the American electorate. Ironically, just a few days after the media mistakenly reported he dropped out of the presidential race, his campaign succeeded in winning "80 percent of the delegates going to the Republican National Convention from Minnesota."[134]

The media also tried to paint the Paul forces as causing trouble or being confrontational, but it was clear that the Paul supporters' objectives focused on attaining more delegates to assist the man they supported. Naturally, their wins and actions in getting to those victories might upset some of the various state Republican Party organizations. "This inevitably

---

[132] "Ron Paul storms off set after CNN keeps asking newsletter questions," http://www.theblaze.com/stories/, December 21, 2011.

[133] Joseph Coleman, "Ron Paul: The invisible candidate?", Yahoo Voices, http://voices.yahoo.com, January 27, 2012.

[134] Tom Mullen, "Republican Party blocking massive Ron Paul event in Tampa?", Washington Times, http://communities.washingtontimes.com, June 2, 2012.

DEBORAH K. SMARTH

has led to some angry clashes with more traditional Republicans, many of whom have been surprised to suddenly find themselves outvoted in organizations they've controlled in the past."[135] The Paul supporters "have been maligned, dismissed, made fun of, ignored and browbeaten for months—years in fact, as they suffered from similar punishments during Ron Paul's 2008 campaign."[136]

What about when the media disseminated the wrong information about Paul not having the plurality of delegates in five states, nearing the convention in Tampa? That happened too, sending out misinformation to the general public despite the Twitter, blogs, and other public comments offered by those following the campaign who knew better. Despite the increased successes and the fact that Paul had succeeded in capturing more than five states' plurality of delegates—enough to put his name in nomination at the convention—there were several media reports that suggested otherwise. As reported by the *Examiner* in July 2012, "the establishment and its media are going with the new reality that Paul actually still needs one more state and Saturday's upcoming Nebraska state convention may be Paul's 'last hope.'"[137] NBC's Anthony Terrell in a post for MSNBC, specifically reported that if Paul's "team can't secure enough delegates [in Nebraska], his longshot bid for the Republican presidential nomination is formally dead." [138] Another news reporter of the Houston Chronicle on July 16 cited that "Paul had the support of four states Louisiana, Iowa, Maine and Minnesota but reported that without Nebraska, it left Paul 'one state short' of the needed five states delegations."[139] Additional mainstream media, like ABC news, carried the same story. Yet as early as May 2012, other non-mainstream media outlets were reporting that Dr. Paul had actually won at least eleven states at

---

[135] Peter Grier, "Are some Ron Paul supporters going rogue?", Christian Science Monitor, http://www.csmonitor.com, May 16, 2012.

[136] Connor Adams Sheets, "Ron Paul 2012 will get 20 delegates in Iowa, predicts prominent Romney supporter," International Business Times, www.ibtimes.com, May 3, 2012.

[137] Jeffrey Phelps, "Media playing RNC ballot charades," http://www.examiner.com, July 9, 2012.

[138] Anthony Terrell, "Ron Paul's last stand," MSNBC, http://firstread.nbcnews.com, July 9, 2012.

[139] Stewart Powell, "Ron Paul misses cut to address delegates at Tampa convention," http://www.startribune.com/politics, July 16, 2012.

that point, exceeding the required totals needed to be on the Republican National Convention's first ballot. More importantly, on July 16, 2012, according to the Facebook page of Ben Swann of Fox 19 Cincinnati, the RNC itself admitted that Paul had already attained the needed goal of a five-state delegate plurality. Interviewed by Kurt Wallace of the *Daily Paul Radio* show, Swann further provided details about these circumstances and developments, something about which the mainstream media was unwilling or incapable of reporting to the public at large.

There were sometimes exceptions to the media blackout. For instance, a transcript from *Democracy Now* broadcast through NPR and hosted by Amy Goodman shows Nermeen Shaikh, reporting from the Republican National Convention floor, documenting "a major eruption of fury" at the convention as the nomination process began when part of the Maine delegation "stormed off the floor in protest against a decision to strip away half of the state's Ron Paul delegates." Amy Goodman cited the fact that the RNC replaced ten of the twenty Paul delegates, "enough to prevent Ron Paul from being nominated from the floor."[140] In the early part of 2012, Paul was referred to as "one of the only remaining candidates who can compete with Romney in the race for cash, largely due to his national base of ardent supporters. That poses a problem for any candidate looking to quickly lock up the nomination."[141] The public received conflicting information from the news media contributing to confusion among voters.

A member of the media from *Business Insider*, a publication which regularly reported on Ron Paul's campaign and candidacy, wrote an article addressing Paul's supporters' contentions about the media blackout. He commented that the publication "can't write about him enough." The article further explains that "every time we publish something about Ron Paul, we are reminded that Ron Paul is, if not President of the United States, at least President of the Internet. The Internet just can't get enough of him." While the reporter comments that despite the fact that Paul polled okay in the early primaries and that "some of our readers are completely bananas about him . . . . There's just no way Ron Paul can win

---

[140] Transcript. "Chaos on the Convention Floor as RNC Blocks Ron Paul Delegates, Alters Seating Rules," Democracy Now, http://www.democracynow.org, August 29, 2012.

[141] Ryan Grim. "New Hampshire primary results: Ron Paul comes in second," Huffington Post, http://www.huffingtonpost.com, January 10, 2012.

the Presidency." He answers that proposition by saying that Paul is "just too extreme." Then he explains that Paul's positions on killing the Federal Reserve, cutting one trillion of government spending, ending all foreign interventions, etc., are not going to be supported by "mainstream voters." He ends his article by saying the media doesn't "think he has a prayer of winning."[142]

Romney was always slated to win the popular vote, if you believe the mainstream media line. Reporting that observation over and over again provided the appearance that Ron Paul just wasn't a factor, and that type of subjective reporting continued throughout the long campaign. A member of the *Wall Street Journal* editorial board had an op-ed piece published which not only demonized Paul's foreign policy positions and certain answers he gave during a presidential debate concerning Iran and 9/11, but actually stated, "Most of Dr. Paul's supporters, of course, don't actually imagine he can become president. Nor do they dwell on the implications of the enlarged influence conferred on him by a few early primary victories . . ."[143] Then take, for instance, the statement which appeared by a staff writer at the Dubuque Telegraph in Iowa: "Ron Paul might not be a factor anymore in the 2012 presidential campaign but his supporters continue to work on the ground level . . ."[144] What kind of reporting and message did this—along with other similar biases in news accounts—send to the general electorate prior to the national convention? If anything, it confused the public and led many to think that Paul was a non-factor in the lead-up to the Republican nomination when, in fact, it was not the case at all!

Interestingly, Joe Scarborough, who hosts the daily MSNBC early morning political talk show *Morning Joe*, who had invited presidential candidate Paul for several interviews on the show, went public—as reported in the publication *Politico*—that he cast his vote for Congressman Ron Paul in the Florida Republican presidential primary. Unlike many other members of the press in the mainstream media who

---

[142]  Henry Blodget, "Dear Ron Paul supporters: Here's the truth about the 'media blackout," Business Insider, http://www.businessinsider.com, January 9, 2012.

[143]  Dorothy Rabinowitz, "What Ron Paul thinks of America," Wall Street Journal, http://online.wsj.com/article, December 22, 2011.

[144]  Erin Murphy, "Ron Paul supporters making some headway," Dubuque Telegraph, http://thonline.com/news/tri-state/article, April 27, 2012.

denied a truthful and thorough discussion of Dr. Paul's policy planks as presidential candidate, it was encouraging to see Scarborough publicly claim that he indeed voted for Paul because he felt Paul was the only authentic Conservative candidate who was addressing real issues with specific solutions concerning the national debt, the Federal Reserve monetary policies, less foreign engagement, and undeclared wars while maintaining a strong defense.

Even though Scarborough personally voted for Paul, he still seemed to follow in the footsteps of the other corporate media when it came to commentary on Paul's presidential candidacy. In the last segment of Scarborough's show on June 20, 2012, Sam Stein ambushed Paul, suggesting that Paul was hypocritical concerning his position on social security. Paul's position in the campaign was to phase out social security, but it does not ask people who have paid into the system to forego their benefits. Stein questioned Paul on social security, trying to make it look like Paul wasn't holding to pure Libertarian views when it came to social security because he himself receives social security payments, yet Paul had said young people should be able to opt out of social security. But Paul also indicated that if people opt out, then they would not be taxed to support social security. "The media don't have to agree with Ron Paul's positions on the issues, but misrepresenting them this way is cheap pandering to the basest emotions of their audience. Paul may be a lot of things, but one thing he is not is a hypocrite. MSNBC and *Morning Joe* should admit that they did their audience a disservice by suggesting that he is."[145]

The Ron Paul Revolution PAC, headed by former CIA intelligence officer Michael Scheuer, had a website which was useful for voters' perusal. The website said, "The mainstream media has crowned Mitt Romney as the GOP nominee for the 2012 election and have declared that he is now moving onto the 'real race.' The mainstream media is doing its job promoting the status quo and now that the choice has been made by those that really know what is going on we can all relax and get back to trusting government in all things. EXCEPT for the inconvenient

---

[145] Tom Mullen, "Morning Joe wrong on Ron Paul and social security," Washington Times, http://communities.washingtontimes.com, June 21, 2012.

DEBORAH K. SMARTH

fact that as caucus states are progressing to their county, district and state conventions Ron Paul supporters are doing very well."[146]

Commenting further about how Paul's candidacy was handled by the media, Scheuer said, "Ron Paul's treatment by mainstream media, other Republican hopefuls, and the punditry makes me think the W.B. Yeats lines 'Things fall apart; the center cannot hold; mere anarchy is loosed upon the world' also describe the year 2012 in the United States. Indeed, Paul's experience in the nomination campaign suggests U.S. politics lacks reasoned substance, common sense, and an understanding of what America's Founding Fathers intended."[147]

Posted on the Daily Paul Internet site on July 24, 2012, a *New York Times* reporter "openly admitted that virtually every major mainstream news organization allows government bureaucrats and campaign officials to censor their stories." Gatekeepers in both the Obama and Romney campaigns approved quotes before they were used in news stories and the same applies for government spokespersons; before using quotes in a story, the gatekeeper approves for the media to use.[148] Once again, this type of control only further indicates that the free and independent press that our Founding Fathers saw as a necessary component in a republican form of government and representative democracy is surely eroding.

The bias and failure to provide full coverage of Ron Paul's presidential candidacy indeed provided preconceived notions about Paul that did not reflect reality. Paul's delegates' state convention wins and prior strong showings in various primary and caucus elections were not fully reported or were the many anomalies and alleged fraud that occurred with regard to final vote tallies in those early primaries and caucuses. In many ways, the electorate's knowledge and understanding of candidate Paul was lacking due to unfair and poor media coverage, and that inevitably

---

[146]  Connor Adams Sheets, "Ron Paul 2012: Can he beat Mitt Romney now that Newt Gingrich is bowing out?", International Business Times, http://www.ibtimes.com, April 25, 2012.

[147]  Michael Scheuer, "President Ron Paul: Ron Paul may be a long shot in November, but he's America's best bet on foreign policy," http://www.foreignpolicy.com, May 3, 2012.

[148]  Michael Snyder, "The New York Times admits that virtually every major news organization allows the news to be censored by government officials," http://endoftheamericandream.com/archives/the-new-york-times, July 23, 2012.

prevented the Paul campaign's ability to capitalize on his strong showings and delegate wins in many state GOP conventions leading to the national GOP convention.

On the whole, the major media networks did not, in fact, report on all the developments at the national convention in Tampa or elevate the issues at hand to the level of coverage they rightfully deserved. Why not? The Republican Party leadership's and Romney campaign's efforts to change the rules so that Paul's name could not be placed in nomination should have turned heads! The major media also did not provide appropriate coverage about Paul's delegates being de-credentialed due to tactical maneuvers by the party establishment, which wanted to prevent any surprises from happening on the convention floor.

Continuing through 2013, the media still does not reference the Paul factor despite the fact that he was indeed the last standing challenger to Mitt Romney in the Republican nomination process. Ironically, in the aftermath of the 2012 post-election analysis report by the RNC issued in March 2013, the publication *Politico* completely eliminates reference to Ron Paul in its discussion about the many 2012 presidential debates held. The article reads, "There were 20 debates in the 2012 cycle, contributing to a rotating series of front-runners, as the anti-Romney baton was handed from Rick Perry to Herman Cain to Rick Santorum to Newt Gingrich."[149]

The major media, for the most part, did not do its job effectively using the highest standards of journalism as their guiding post for reporting. It is truly amazing that the members of the press did not inform the general public about these important events and occurrences surrounding the nomination process. Why wouldn't the public want to know about the party's unfair and unethical treatment of duly elected state delegates and rule changes affecting the Paul delegates' numbers? After all, these kinds of actions did prevent the possibility of Ron Paul's name going in nomination. The mainstream media outlets did not bolster a fair and open democratic process! As Paul's campaign senior advisor, Doug Wead said, many months after the campaign had ended, "The AP (Associated Press) virtually led the national media in their censorship and

---

[149] Kevin Robillard, "Reince Prieebus: No more traveling circus," Politico, http://www.politico.com, March 22, 2013.

misreporting of the Ron Paul presidential campaign in 2012." [150]At times throughout the long presidential primary campaign on up to Tampa, one had to question the existence of a free press. Sadly, the media did not do its job, and it appears that reporting trends of this nature continue to go in this direction today.

In many instances, the American people had fallen prey to media manipulation and misinformation during the 2012 presidential campaign. A free and truthful press and a truly informed electorate are the only means to a fully democratic process. Only under these conditions in combination with fair and transparent elections can the citizens truly control election outcomes. Unfortunately, the party establishment's GOP nomination process and a biased mass media failed these litmus tests.

---

[150] Doug Wead, "The media's shock over IRS scandal," World Net Daily, http://www.wnd.com/2013/05, May 22, 2013.

# CHAPTER FOUR

# Post-Tampa Convention, Election Day, and Its Aftermath

F OLLOWING THE NATIONAL convention, the rule changes left a bad taste among not only Ron Paul supporters, but also Tea Party groups and other Conservatives, many of whom voiced their opposition. One alternate delegate, Neil Lynch from Maple Grove, Minnesota, commenting on the rules governing delegates selection, said, "They turned it from a bottom-up process that it has been in most states, to a top-down system where the party leadership—based on who they determine is the ordained nominee—will be able to not only control the delegations but also vet the delegates themselves. They will be able to keep the people they like and kick out the people they don't like."[151]

After the Tampa national GOP convention, Ron Paul thanked all his supporters. In a September 2012 message, he said, "Your support has made an incredible impact that will continue on well into the future. In fact, as I look back at the past year, I'm literally amazed at how far we've come . . . . Due to our Liberty Movement's youth, energy, and growing numbers, establishment Republicans are recognizing their days of controlling the national GOP are coming to an end. Even now, they are being forced to recognize that our issues—like finally auditing the Federal Reserve—are not going away. My hope, with your continued support, it will not end until free markets, sound money, constitutional principles,

---

[151] Mark Maley, "Ron Paul supporters fear GOP is trying to quash grassroots movement," http://www.burnsville.patch.com/groups/politics-and-elections, September 4, 2012.

Following the rule changes at the national convention to eliminate grassroots participation, some state Republican parties took action. For instance, the New Hampshire Republicans held a convention at the end of September 2012, and they unanimously passed a resolution by voice vote, "rebuking the national GOP for the rules changes" made in Tampa. Specifically, the resolution cites that the changes made to Rule 12 gives "unprecedented power to the national committee to change party rules without the input and approval of state parties and their members."[155] As reported in www.nashua.patch.com, some observers believe that the vote "may have been as many as 90 percent of those present, reflects the growing influence of the Republican Liberty movement in New Hampshire." The resolution was hailed as a "courageous step to reclaim the GOP for the grassroots."

Hamdan Azhar, a Paul supporter participating at the national convention, indicated that a Romney delegate stated to him, "You have to give Ron Paul credit for bringing all these young people into the party . . . It's a shame the party hasn't been more welcoming."[156]

In a Fox News interview with Sean Hannity, participating on a panel, Max Pappas—vice president of Public Policy and Government Affairs at the Conservative group FreedomWorks—said, "I think you have one element out there that's going to be pretty important, that's where are the Ron Paul guys gonna go. And Romney needs the Ron Paul guys if he's gonna win." As an *International Business Times* article noted, "Pappas makes an interesting point when he suggests that Ron Paul supporters are so vital to Mitt Romney's 2012 campaign hopes. Paul has tens of thousands of strident supporters, and many of them say they will not vote for Romney or Obama if Paul is not on the ballot, as they believe they are two sides of the same plutocratic, corporate-run coin."[157] In addition, Pappas stated that "Romney needs to pick someone [for vice president] that will make Ron Paul supporters happy if he wants to have any chance

---

[155] "New Hampshire Republicans defy the establishment," http://www.dailypaul.com, October 1, 2012.

[156] Hamdan Azhar, "Love and Politics: Why I'm voting for Ron Paul," PolicyMic, http://www.policymic.com, November 4, 2012.

[157] Connor Adams Sheets, "Ron Paul supporters essential to Mitt Romney candidacy, Fox News Guest Says (Video)," International Business Times, http://www.ibtimes.com, July 16, 2012.

of beating President Barack Obama when voters head to the polls in November."

Responding to that panel discussion on Fox, a strong Paul backer named Mat Larson, who became widely known for his Internet video updates on the status of Ron Paul's candidacy, explained on video that Paul supporters are "not just tow-the-party-liners . . . . Romney is Obama, so why would we vote for him, too. At some point of time in his career he has been exactly like Obama. And that is the scary part."

The article explains that during the Fox panel exchanges, the subject of vice president is raised, and Hannity asks, "Who will it be, who should it be?" Clearly, the subject of vice president selection should have taken into consideration the Paul supporters' philosophical leanings and principles. Ultimately, the Paul Ryan selection upon closer scrutiny would not attract Ron Paul supporters.

As the founder of the New Hampshire Tea Party Coalition, Jane Aitken noted in a published column, there were "at least two, if not more, factions of tea partiers" who attended the convention as well as rallies, and none of them wanted Romney. Romney's pick for vice president, as one liberty activist suggested, was an "imitation Ron Paul." They maintained that Paul Ryan is no real Conservative or constitutionalist. For instance, Aitken pointed out in her column that Ryan voted for the TARP bailout in 2008, voted for the Economic Stimulus (2008), the bailout of GM and Chrysler and an additional $192 billion in anti-recession stimulus spending (2009), voted for "No Child Left Behind," and voted for the $400 billion Medicare package. He also voted for making the Patriot Act permanent (2005) and for allowing electronic surveillance without a warrant (2006). In addition, concerning war and intervention abroad, he voted to authorize military force in Iraq (2002), voted for an emergency appropriation of $78 billion for the Iraq and Afghanistan mobilizations (2003), supported declaring Iraq part of the War on Terror with no exit date, and voted against taking U.S. troops out of Iraq within ninety days (May 2007). Even Fox commentator Neil Cavuto, who oftentimes interviewed Ron Paul throughout the campaign, called Ryan's proposed budget "mild" compared to Ron Paul's.

According to a news account, Ron Paul even noted that there is such a small difference in the proposed $3.5 trillion congressional budget versus Obama's $3.8 trillion budget that the rhetoric being used by politicians is not even justified. In fact, Paul noted that even under the most optimistic scenarios the supposed radical plan does not balance the federal budget until his one-year-old great-granddaughter will be in college. Under less optimistic assumptions, he said that his great-granddaughter will be almost thirty before she sees a balanced federal budget, pointing out that it will occur only if Congress adheres to the current budget in future years, a skeptical assumption since future congresses cannot be bound to current spending plans.

On the campaign trail in September 2012, vice presidential candidate Paul Ryan, at a town hall event in Lima, Ohio, was asked by an attendee why supporters of Ron Paul should back the Republican ticket. As reported in an October 12, 2012, *New York Daily News* column, Ryan was offended by the comment and shouted back, "Do you want Barack Obama re-elected?" He further claimed that Ron Paul is actually a "friend." That couldn't have been farther from the truth! Yet at the Ohio event, Ryan did give credit to Paul concerning his crusade to audit the Federal Reserve and that all this money printing by that entity "risks debasing our currency . . . undermining the value of the dollar." Ron Paul was one of only three House Republican members who did not endorse the Romney ticket. It should be pointed out that advisors to Romney included the same Neoconservatives that advised President George W. Bush, like John Bolton and Dan Senor. Dick Cheney's daughter, Liz Cheney, took part in weekly conference calls with the campaign. Ron Paul, on the other hand, unflinchingly opposed aggressive wars.

In the end, Obama received 65,899,660 votes or 51.1 percent of the popular vote with 332 electoral votes, while Romney yielded 60,932,152 votes or 47.2 percent of the popular vote with 206 electoral votes. The margin of loss was 3.9 percent.[158] According to a *National Review* analysis, Obama had 6 percent fewer votes in 2012 than in 2008, while Romney received 1 percent more votes than McCain had received in 2008. Libertarian candidate and former New Mexico governor Gary Johnson received 1,275,951, 1 percent of the vote.[159] Other third-party candidates received a little less than a million votes. The *National Review* article cited that compared to prior presidential election cycles in which voter turnout had increased by 16 percent between 2000 and 2004, the

[158] http://en.wikipedia.org/wiki/United_States_Presidential_Election_2012.

[159] http://en.wikipedia.org/wiki/United_States_Presidential_Election_2012.

2012 presidential election turnout was about 2 percent less than in 2008, falling from 131 million to about 128 million.[160]

Romney, who thought he would win the presidential election, commented post-election by saying to donors during a telephone town hall, "The Obama campaign was following the old playbook of giving a lot of stuff to groups that they hoped they could get to vote for them and be motivated to go out to the polls, specifically the African American community, the Hispanic community and young people . . . In each case they were very generous in what they gave to those groups."[161] His comments drew fire from those within Romney's own party, and he received criticism in general.

However, several million fewer Americans did not show up and cast their vote at the ballot box in 2012 than in 2008. Apparently, many voters did not feel motivated enough by the choices they had between the two major party candidates, Mitt Romney and incumbent President Barack Obama. During commonplace talk, people genuinely seemed unexcited about either party's nominee!

During the GOP primary and caucus season, Ron Paul won over two million votes, taking on the establishment and party power structure with his assault on the Federal Reserve, his strong anti-war stance and opposition to covert assassinations, and the Obama administration's secret "Kill List" reported on in the *New York Times* and editorialized against by Fox News judicial analyst and commentator, Judge Andrew Napolitano.

Even though the Libertarian presidential candidate, former governor of New Mexico Gary Johnson (who announced his candidacy after it was apparent that Paul did not obtain the long—shot nomination) held some similar positions to Republican presidential candidate Ron Paul, Johnson received only 1 percent of the general electorate's cast votes. He was not Ron Paul and certainly did not have the resources that Ron Paul had during his grassroots campaign and in the lead-up to the national convention in Tampa.

After failing to clinch, the 2012 Republican nomination, many supporters of Paul exchanged dialogue concerning their uncertainty as to

---

[160] Michael Barone, "Obama 2012 and Bush 2004: How two presidents hung on for re-election," National Review, http://www.nationalreview.com/article/336474, December 27, 2012.

[161] Paul Whitefield, "Mitt Romney and Ron Paul: Who had the better exit lines?", Los Angeles Times, http://www.latimes.com, November 15, 2012.

who to support in the general election. Some may have voted for Romney even though his views were far away from their true candidate, Ron Paul. Others decided to write-in Dr. Paul's name on the November ballot. Some supported Libertarian Party's nominee, Gary Johnson. Yet others just stayed home.

And there are stories and letters to the editor that showed the decision-making process of Paul supporters. Take, for instance, the one that appeared in the *Sioux City Journal* on October 28, 2012, by Carl Hardy, who wrote, "After careful consideration, listening to the debates, watching the endless TV ads, and reading numerous editorials supporting both sides . . . neither candidate, Barack Obama or Mitt Romney, deserve my vote . . . . My choice from the start continues to be Ron Paul. Unfortunately, Mr. Paul is not on the ticket because Americans are blind and the majority did not take time to listen to his positive, well-thought-out decisions on the economy, foreign policy . . . and a wide variety of other important issues. My vote is a write-in for Ron Paul."

It must be remembered what Ron Paul said to his many millions of supporters across America, "We must remember, elections are short-term efforts. Revolutions are long-term projects." Paul's revolution, which evolved even more strongly throughout the course of the 2012 presidential campaign, focused on a revolution of ideas and the way people think. Spreading the truth and making government the servant of the people, working for the people's good.

So it was and remains the goal of many Ron Paul supporters to work and influence the Republican Party to include a larger tent of persons and to continue to participate from the bottom up and use it to expand influence within the Republican Party at all levels of government. It must be remembered that Paul brought into the party the youngest delegation ever at the national convention. They were not CEOs, wealthy or political patronage folks, and lawyers, just ordinary people from different walks of life, including teachers, actors, techies, college students, etc.

Certainly, the treatment they received at the Tampa convention gave impetus and further passion for moving ahead and strengthening the cause of the Liberty wing of the party. The unraveling of events, the unfairness that exhibited itself from the state conventions through the national convention actually seem to have further invigorated Paul supporters.

While the national party debated about the reasons why it lost to Obama in the 2012 November election, they mostly focused on narrow explanations, such as women and Latino voters, media bias, poor campaign messaging, extremism of the Tea Party, moderate candidate Romney, New Jersey governor Chris Christie engaging with President Obama on Hurricane Sandy immediately prior to election Tuesday. But will the Republicans learn that their party positions on some very important issues—domestic and foreign policy—could truly be the real culprits in their election loss? That remains to be seen.

Statist policies are not what are needed. Regardless of who won, the same statist policies are in place currently. Paul's attraction to millions of voters and activist supporters relates to his rejection of status quo solutions and platforms. Paul supporters found it ironic that Republican strategist Karl Rove commented on Fox News about the president "suppressing the vote."

Yet Paul delegates and supporters found themselves systematically shut out of the process by rule abuses and other shenanigans at individual GOP state conventions and at the national convention in Tampa, not to forget the alleged manipulation of voting outcomes in primary and caucus elections early in the presidential primary campaign season prior to the GOP state conventions.

Some contend that even if the arduous research process of analyzing and reaching conclusive evidence that the Ron Paul supporters tipped the election by either not voting at all, wrote-in Ron Paul's name, or voted for a third-party candidate, "There is also no guarantee any accurate results from the findings would ever be publicized. Establishment Republican operatives could manipulate the data to either prove Ron Paul 'cost' the GOP the 2012 Presidential Election, or continue to dismiss him as a 'non-factor' as was done throughout the Republican Primaries and at the Republican National Convention."[162] But it is interesting to note that according to statistics put together for PolicyMic by Hamdan Azhar, a Ron Paul supporter who is a data scientist and freelance writer, the analysis indicates that "in no less than five states, Romney's margin of loss to President Obama in the general election was less than the number of votes received by Ron Paul in that state's primary."[163] Those states included Florida, New Hampshire, Ohio, and Virginia. The findings

---

[162]  Brian Cole, "Third-party and Ron Paul voters impact Election Day," http://www.examiner.com, November 7, 2012.

[163]  Gregory Patin, "The Ron Paul factor in the GOP's defeat," http://www.examiner.com, November 10, 2012.

reveal that those four states accounted for 64 electoral votes. The analysis maintains if those 64 votes had gone to the Republican candidate, then Obama would not have received 332 electoral votes, and that is the difference. For a presidential candidate to become president, 270 electoral votes are needed. Despite these interesting observations, it is safe to assume that not all Paul primary voters would have voted for the GOP candidate, especially because there were stark differences between Paul and Romney.

The fact remains that Ron Paul had attracted Republican Conservatives, progressive Democrats disenchanted with Obama, and Independents. Many Independents liked the fact that Ron Paul "refused to play along with the political system." While most of the American electorate was not privy to many polls in 2012 during the nomination process, the Paul campaign did underscore at different intervals during the campaign trail that polling showed Ron Paul ahead of Obama in many instances, and in others, Paul was in a dead heat.

Despite the overall poor results for the GOP, Republican candidates who supported Campaign for Liberty issues, like Congressman Justin Amash (Michigan), won re-election in a tough race; Congressman-elect Kerry Bentivolio (Michigan), former Congressman Steve Stockman (Texas), and Senator-elect Ted Cruz (Texas) as well as Thomas Massie (Kentucky) were victorious. It could be the beginning of a real movement that incrementally wins more seats in Congress. It was also reported that Paul's followers also picked up seats in Florida and Georgia.

In January 2013, two of Paul's top 2012 Iowa caucus campaign aides were re-elected as chairman and vice chairman of Iowa's state Republican Party, joining the ranks of Nevada Paul supporters elected to two spots on the Republican National Committee in 2012. Paul backers have been reported as making inroads in Colorado, Florida, Louisiana, Maine, Minnesota, and Missouri "in part vestiges of his 2012 presidential campaign." Despite those strides, it was reported that a Maine Ron Paul supporter, Mark Willis, who was a representative to the Republican National Committee, said that national party leaders were "running a smear campaign to oust him from the committee, even as he wages his own longshot bid to become the national Party's next chairman." At the national convention, he lost his seat as a delegate in Tampa because of his outspoken support for candidate Ron Paul. All the questions being raised about Willis ironically came a week prior to the challenge he intended to launch against current RNC chairman Reince Priebus. The party alleged that failure to support the party's presidential nominee was grounds for removal from the committee. Willis said he knew of two RNC members in Maine who Priebus contacted about the issue.[164] Priebus, of course, was re-elected Republican National Committee chairman.

Realizing its need to turn the corner, the Republican Party, which kicked off its winter strategy session in Charlotte, North Carolina in January 2013, launched a website to solicit ideas and constructive input about what the party did wrong in 2012 and what steps to take to improve itself. President Obama won 332 Electoral College votes and drew support from "more than 70 percent of Hispanic and more than 95 percent of Black voters."[165] In addition, "according to exit polls conducted during the November election, Obama outperformed Romney among younger voters."

"Fully half of voters who backed the Democratic president were under age 45, compared with 40 percent of Romney's supporters." When looking at age by party, 49 percent of Democratic voters were age forty-four or younger contrasted to 42 percent of Republican voters. According to the Associated Press, the gap proved greater in the ten most closely divided states.[166] Based on some of these observations, it would appear that the GOP should do more to embrace the youth that came into the party as a result of Dr. Paul's efforts and the positions on issues to which his young supporters were strongly drawn.

Stories like the one by Ani DeGroot, the youngest national delegate from Iowa to the RNC, personify why Dr. Paul's following is so strong. In 2007, Ani went to her astrophysics class and noticed scribbled letters on the blackboard, saying, "Google Ron Paul!" She acknowledged she thought he might be an astrophysicist or a scientist. But then she Googled Paul's name, and she acquiesces that he "was something that would eventually change my life." She noted in her account for Yahoo News, "As I read more on Dr. Paul, I encountered for the first time someone in

---

[164] Kevin Miller, "Maine Ron Paul supporter fears he's being smeared," Portland Press Herald, http://www.pressherald.com/news, January 18, 2013.

[165] Chris Moody, "The Republican Party seeks to learn from its mistakes—and it wants your help," Yahoo News, http://news.yahoo.com/blogs/ticket, January 23, 2013.

[166] Thomas Beaumont, "Ron Paul's Republican legacy growing in caucus states like Iowa and Nevada," Huffington Post, http://www.huffingtonpost.com, January 15, 2013.

politics who employed logic consistently throughout his policy positions and adhered to his principles strongly. As my own political philosophy developed, I soon came to the conclusion that the libertarian philosophy was indeed the only political ideology rooted in logic throughout its entire application."[167] She said that encountering Ron Paul and her subsequent research led her to leave the field of natural sciences and focus her studies in political science and economics. She then became an activist in the campus's Young Americans for Liberty (YAL) chapter and ultimately participated in the 2012 Ron Paul presidential campaign.

During the nomination campaign, "Paul drew blockbuster crowds while on college campuses" and "carried a higher percentage of younger voters than Romney." A Ron Paul supporter was quoted as saying on a Libertarian blog, "I want to make sure that when the Republican Party loses, terribly . . . I want [them to know] it's because they systematically shut out the most intelligent, most youthful and active voting bloc in American history."[168] Paul consistently attracted a high percentage of the youth vote throughout his campaign.

In fact, in highlighting what were considered to be important tasks for the Paul forces to undertake at the convention, one of three aspects included the fact that the Paul delegates should continue to provide "a reminder that the 2 to 4 million Paul supporters in the hinterland may be needed to defeat Obama."[169] Yet obviously the Republican leadership did not heed these messages or grasp the importance of these new emerging activists that Ron Paul had brought into the party during the state convention process or the national convention.

On March 18, 2013, the Republican National Committee issued its one-hundred-page report providing a post-election analysis of the party's defeat in the 2012 presidential election. The document, formally known as the Growth and Opportunity Project, is referred to in political circles as its 2012 "autopsy" report. The report was described as "essentially an establishment Republican whitewash of the party's abject failure in the

---

[167] Ani DeGroot, "From Astrophysics to politics and a change in philosophy," http://news.yahoo.com, April 3, 2013.

[168] Gregory Patin, "The Ron Paul factor in the GOP's defeat," http://www.examiner.com, November 10, 2012.

[169] Jeff Taylor, "The GOP has a long tradition—of open disagreement at the convention," American Conservative, http://www.theamericanconservative.com, July 16, 2012.

2012 elections."[170] Instead of learning from its terrible actions taken against grassroots Paul supporters and heeding the reactions of other delegates who opposed the RNC rule changes at the national convention in Tampa, it appears that the national GOP contends that it just needs to market itself better, enhance messaging and campaign mechanics driven by a culture based on data, technology, analytics, and the like. "The report also calls for a shorter primary season and fewer debates."[171] Of course, this would prevent insurgent candidates, like Ron Paul, from ever emerging and obtaining strong grassroots support. "On almost every issue, the report addresses—minority outreach, the primary schedule, and the importance of quantitative analysis over conservative gut checks—the RNC autopsy reads like the party establishment's manual for reasserting its control over the party."[172] Priebus, the RNC national chairman, commented on MSNBC's *Morning Joe*, that he didn't think it served the party well to have the GOP presidential candidates "running around in a traveling circus and doing 23 debates."[173]

The non-profit entity, Campaign for Liberty, also indicates that the Task Force report made recommendations like requiring every state to hold primaries rather than caucuses and conventions. This requirement puts grassroots candidates at a disadvantage since primaries rely on multi-million dollar advertising campaigns as opposed to grassroots organization volunteers and donors for caucuses and conventions. The report also references holding regional primaries to replace individual state primaries; this approach would also favor well-funded establishment candidates to run "multiple state campaigns at once." Another recommendation called for the GOP to control primary debates, guaranteeing an advantage to party-preferred and establishment candidates while grassroots, populist candidates would be "shut out." John Tate, president of Campaign for Liberty, says that these recommendations

---

[170] Steven Holmes, "GOP election 'autopsy' report is establishment Republicans blaming conservatives," http://www.examiner.com, March 19, 2013.

[171] John Dickerson, "Habeas GOP/The Republican Party's autopsy of the 2012 loss puts political expediency over principles," http://www.slate.com, March 18, 2013.

[172] Ibid.

[173] Kevin Robillard, "Reince Priebus: No more 'traveling circus,'" Politico, http://www.Politico.com, March 22, 2013.

DEBORAH K. SMARTH

are "designed to cement the establishment's control over picking the nominee in 2016."[174]

The conclusions of the report are not surprising, given the fact that the Task Force, which developed the report, consisted of establishment Republicans! For instance, President George Bush's press secretary Ari Fleischer, Henry Barbour, a nephew of former Republican governor Haley Barbour (Mississippi), and other establishment connected people were part of this task force.

Following the issuance of its March election analysis report, the Republican National Committee held its spring meeting April 10-13, 2013, in Los Angeles, California. Virginia RNC committeeman Morton Blackwell, a longtime Conservative on the Rules Committee, who spearheaded opposition to the change in rules at the August 2012 national GOP convention in Tampa, also played a role at the RNC spring meeting. He attempted to repeal the rules that were adopted in Tampa. Supporters and delegates of Ron Paul joined together with other traditional Conservatives to try and repeal the 2012 rule changes backed and pushed by the Romney campaign. The rules adopted in Tampa promoted winner-take-all primaries. In so doing, it discouraged giving too much power to grassroots activists in the state convention process in selecting the GOP presidential nominee. The president of Campaign for Liberty John Tate noted that the rules adopted in August 2012 in Tampa were "designed to hand even more control to party insiders, fat-cat donors, and GOP hack consultants."[175]

Prior to the start of the RNC spring meeting, Morton Blackwell wrote to RNC chairman Reince Priebus, saying that "the power grab initiated by Ben Ginsberg at the Convention Rules Committee outraged many RNC members and millions of grassroots Republicans across the country. It caused thunderous opposition when the Convention Rules Committee report was presented to the National Convention in Tampa."[176] Sixty key Conservative leaders, like Edwin Meese III, Gary Bauer, and Phyllis Schlafly, joined in urging Priebus to repeal the adopted rules in Tampa. "The action to overturn the rules began with Ron Paul supporters, who argued the changes would have prevented them from voting their

---

[174] John Tate, letter to supporters, April 6, 2013.

[175] John Tate, letter to supporters, April 6, 2013.

[176] "Morton Blackwell: There's a showdown coming at the next RNC meeting," http://www.westernfreepress.com, April 5, 2013.

conscience, and in doing so give Republican insiders more leverage in choosing the nominee."[177]

At the spring meeting, Priebus was quoted as saying, "We all agree the grassroots are the center of this party and are vital to winning elections."[178] But those words did not align with the actions taken at the spring RNC meeting. According to Campaign for Liberty's president John Tate, "Party insiders defeated Morton Blackwell's Resolution from clearing the Rules Committee and making it to the floor for a full vote" of the RNC. Tate also commented, "And when all was said and done, the RNC only overturned one of the many destructive rules passed in Tampa."[179] It was reported by Tate that "the RNC passed a resolution honoring Ron Paul at the spring meeting." Yet in the same breadth the party insiders prevented repeal of all of the rules adopted at the Tampa convention, which discouraged grassroots influence and control over the nomination process. Just as Priebus and the Romney campaign envoys were responsible for initiating the very rules that were adopted in Tampa, which prevented Ron Paul's full delegation from being seated at the convention, the RNC party establishment prevented Blackwell's resolution to repeal all of the adopted rules from passing at the 2013 spring meeting.

FreedomWorks president Matt Kibbe said, "The RNC's spring meeting was just the first skirmish in a fight that can have only one outcome, because the party's insiders are fighting an inevitable cultural trend toward more decentralization, transparency and grassroots participation."[180] It appears that the battle for the soul of the party will continue.

In his fifty minute farewell address to Congress, a body he served in honorably for more than two decades, Ron Paul provided his vision and those arguments propounded during his congressional career and presidential campaigns alike: personal liberty, free markets, simple monetary policy, minimal taxation, personal responsibility over welfare, and a limited government. The *Huffington Post* noted, "But Paul also spoke about many of his views that have made him a thorn in the side of his Republican colleagues, as well as a fascinating and influential

---

[177] David Yonkman, "GOP activists win battle at RNC spring meeting," Newsmax, http://www.newsmax.com, April 12, 2013.

[178] Ibid.

[179] John Tate, letter to supporters, April 14, 2013.

[180] David Yonkman, op. cit.

DEBORAH K. SMARTH

figure for many others across the political spectrum. His strong defense of civil liberties, opposition to the war on drugs, disapproval of foreign intervention, frustration with the status quo and skepticism of expanding executive power all made appearances in his nearly 50-minute address."[181]

Even though Ron Paul's congressional career has ended as he retired in January 2013, he chairs the non-profit Campaign for Liberty organization, continuing the revolution of ideas to promote the education of Americans on the truth in so many public policy issue areas. As US News reported, "Americans haven't heard the last of libertarian icon Ron Paul. The former Republican presidential candidate, who inspired the most passionate followers of anyone in the 2012 race, says he will continue spreading the word about the need for less government, lower taxes, and fewer U.S. military interventions abroad." [182]

The truthfulness of Paul shines in his continued explanations and proclamations about the irrational policies that the Government pursues oftentimes, both Republicans and Democrats. He has no problem touching upon politically incorrect issues, but that is his draw and an integral part of what made him such an attractive presidential candidate as compared to the typical politician. He was willing to speak truth to power. His millions of supporters liked that character trait, which buoyed his support among regular citizens and further inspired them to be activists on his behalf and the platform for which he stood. He said, "My goal has always been to change people's minds because as long as people demand more government, they will get it. Government reflects the people. That is why I am excited to go to college campuses and I will continue to do that. That's where I will get a lot of support."

While the Republican Party agreed with Paul on his core fiscal policies, they are still resistant to Paul's call for a return to the gold standard and auditing and eventually ending the Federal Reserve System. They also depart on his military and foreign affairs policies. He opposed both the Iraq and Afghanistan wars as well as foreign interventions in Libya and Syria, would like to end all foreign aid, and is against another military intervention with Iran over their supposed attainment of

---

[181]   Nick Wing, "Ron Paul Farewell Speech: What did he get right over the course of his career?" (Video), Huffington Post, http://www.huffingtonpost.com, November 14, 2012.

[182]   Kenneth Walsh, "Ron Paul won't go quietly," US News & World Report, http://www.usnews.com/news/blogs, November 9, 2012.

nuclear weapons. He also opposed the use of unmanned drones. To the Republican Party's own demise, candidate Romney, in the foreign policy debate with President Obama, was seen as "agreeing with Obama's drone use, Iran sanctions and interventionist tendencies."

Michael Scheuer, former Bin Laden CIA unit chief, referred to both Obama and Romney as "interventionist democracy crusaders . . . surrounded by war-mongering Neoconservatives, although those on the Democratic side are more quietly malign."[183] Both Romney's and Obama's pro-interventionist leanings were affirmed in the presidential foreign policy debate.

Viewers of the presidential debate "saw a Republican candidate (Romney) advocating to increase the size of America's already massive military to ensure the nation can always be involved in two military conflicts simultaneously, and they saw both candidates agreeing that America has to find a way to influence the minds and culture of the entire Muslim world." In contradistinction, "Representative Paul would have presented a sharp contrast to the President, condemning his drone-happy policies and reminding him that the 'crippling' sanctions put on Iran are not something to brag about, but an act of war that hurts the country's poor population more than its policy makers."[184] There is no doubt that Paul would have offered sharper policy differences to Obama that are appealing to a large segment of voters.

News organizations commented about the agreements of Romney and Obama on foreign policy following their October debate. For instance, Paul Mulshine, a columnist with a northern Jersey daily newspaper wrote, "But imagine for a second Romney had taken Ron Paul's position. He could have pointed out that Obama has spent four years getting Americans killed in Afghanistan, with nothing whatsoever to show for it . . . . He (Romney) could have stated that we need to stop meddling in the Mideast . . . Instead of taking the Ron Paul view, Romney let himself get led around by the so-called neo-conservatives."[185] It was apparent in

---

[183]   Michael Scheuer, "No Matter who wins, the next president will—without question—be an interventionist war president," http://www.non-intervention.com, November 5, 2012.

[184]   Michael Priebe, "Are there any Ron Paul Republicans left in October," http://www.examiner.com, October 25, 2012.

[185]   Paul Mulshine, "The mess Mitt made: He should have listened to Ron Paul on foreign policy," http://blog.nj.com/njv_paul_mulshine/2012/10, October 23, 2012.

fact, it is certainly a legitimate observation to raise the question, "Did the same 'fraud' get perpetrated during the GOP presidential primary debates?" It was apparent, oftentimes, that debate panelists, media, and other tow-the-party-line candidates tried awfully hard to demean the courageous positions of Dr. Paul.

Ron Paul's influence goes beyond the 2012 presidential nominating process, convention, and Election Day. As David Boaz of the Cato Institute stated, "We used to say most people found libertarianism by reading Ayn Rand. In the last five years, most people have found libertarianism by listening to Ron Paul." An editor at *Reason* magazine and historian of this movement, Brian Doherty, also called the Texas Republican, a "miracle." Prior to Paul's emergence as a leader in the Libertarian movement, those who were attracted to that political philosophy "found many admirable traits in political figures like Barry Goldwater and Ronald Reagan . . ."[194]

Ron Paul has made the movement stronger by attracting a greater number of votes, a little more than two million plus, five times more in his 2012 GOP presidential nomination efforts than in his Libertarian Party nominee bid in 1988. Despite the media's dismissiveness and poor reporting in the majority of instances about Paul's essence, he garnered 2,095,795 votes in the primaries and caucuses where his campaign competed.[195] The Paul campaign had decided early on that they would only compete in certain state primaries and caucuses and focus its campaign strategy on laser-targeted GOP state conventions to win as many delegates as possible to the national convention.

A few months prior to the national presidential election, a Hill Poll of 1,000 likely voters conducted on July 26 indicated that 93 percent of likely U.S. voters say "policies and competence" is more important to them than "likeability" when choosing a president; 3 percent say likeability is more important. Yet in the lead-up to the national GOP convention, the presidential candidate who spoke most substantively about national domestic and foreign policy issues, Ron Paul, was not heard by the vast majority of Americans who voted because of a sustained media blackout and poor perception the corporate media was

---

[194] John Harwood, "Libertarian legion stands ready to accept torch from Paul," New York Times, http://www.nytimes.com, August 25, 2012.

[195] http://en.wikipedia.org/wiki/Republican_Party_presidential_primaries_2012.

able to conjure up in its subjective and biased characterizations of Paul's candidacy.

The congressional seniority system and falling into line with party leadership wishes on policy and votes on legislation are often key considerations for chairmanships and moved legislative measures. By those standards, perhaps Ron Paul's congressional career was not as successful. After all, he had no problem voting no, veering oftentimes from the party positions as he was the "conscience" of the U.S. Congress. But the fact that he had a small number of bills passed through the Congress and signed into law, in a way, could be viewed as a badge of honor. It is a known fact that his own party leaders, fellow Texans, and former leaders in the U.S. House of Representatives Tom DeLay and Dick Armey "denied him a coveted committee chairmanship."

Yet Paul "has greater name recognition across the country" than the two U.S. senators from his home state of Texas, Senators Kay Bailey Hutchison and John Cornyn. "Paul received millions more votes in his 2012 Republican presidential campaign than his home state's powerful governor, Rick Perry. He has attracted more campaign contributors than any Texan not named Bush. And he has more Twitter followers than the rest of the Texas congressional delegation combined."[196]

Paul acknowledged upon his retirement from Congress that things are a lot worse from when he took office in his first special election victory in 1976. He states that "our liberties are less. We are in endless wars. The economy is in shambles. And the government is dysfunctional." Paul, though, says he is hopeful because of the tens of thousands of young people who believe and have embraced his message of liberty and who are slowly entering the American political system. He expects to continue to visit campuses across the country in 2013 to speak to the nation's youth. "Outside of Washington, I am very optimistic," says Paul. He kicked off his 2013 college tour at Washington and Lee University in Virginia. He has fueled a national political movement largely through the Internet and has fomented discussions on important aspects of economic, domestic, and foreign policy issues. In 2013, some of the political talk show hosts and commentators are only now beginning to discuss those very issues that presidential campaign contender Ron Paul catalyzed during the long presidential campaign trail. Throughout the long campaign, he

---

[196] Richard S. Dunham, "Paul's quirky congressional career comes to a close," http://www.mysanantonio.com/news/politics, December 29, 2012.

DEBORAH K. SMARTH

consistently talked about constitutional principles, liberties, and freedom and how these are being infringed upon by government actions.

Political science professor at Minnesota's Carleton College, Steven Schier, notes that Ron Paul "is a gadfly and a man of principle" but, because of that his legacy, "is an unusual one for a retiring U.S. representative. His ability to boost a national libertarian movement that will outlive his career is his biggest accomplishment. The modern libertarian movement had no more consequential advocate than Ron Paul."

As reported by RT news on February 14, 2013, Ron Paul will host a daily radio program, providing two commentary segments daily on national radio, which will be broadcast across the country. Beginning March 2013, the public will have the ability to download a weekly podcast of Paul's segments also. Founder Norm Pattiz of Westwood One and Courtside Entertainment Group stated in a press release that "there's no questioning the fact that Ron Paul is one of today's most impactful leaders. His thoughts and opinions have created a significant and loyal following that has made its presence known throughout the country." Paul's daily messages will be aired on an array of networks and on the Web. Concerning this opportunity, Paul said, "Radio and podcasting are a much more powerful means of communication than speaking on the floor of Congress. I welcome this chance to . . . interact with America in a new way, delivering a message that is timelier than ever and a philosophy that people are clearly hungry to hear more about."[197]

In addition to the daily radio program, Paul also announced another new project on April 17, 2013. He has launched a new Institute for Peace and Prosperity. The press release issued about the new effort began with, "The neo-conservative era is dead." The Institute's Board of Advisors includes academia and former and current members of Congress, Representative Walter Jones (R-No. Carolina), Representative John Duncan (R-Tennessee), and former Congressman Dennis Kucinich (D-Ohio). Former CIA intelligence officer Dr. Michael Scheuer also serves on the board as well as economist Llewellyn "Lew" Rockwell Jr. and Senior Judicial Analyst, Fox News Channel, Judge Andrew Napolitano. Freshman Congressman Thomas Massie (R-Kentucky), who attended the press conference announcement, "praised the willingness of

---

[197] "Ron Paul to host daily radio program and podcast," http://rt.com/usa/news, February 14, 2013.

Paul and Kucinich to oppose their party when they felt that they needed to."[198] According to Paul's office, the think tank "will fill the growing demand for information on foreign affairs from a non-interventionist perspective . . . and will provide unique educational opportunities to university students and others." The group hopes to promote a new understanding "that only through a peaceful foreign policy can we hope for a prosperous tomorrow."[199] At the press conference announcement, Paul was quoted as saying rhetorically, "What is life all about? What is wrong with the Golden Rule in foreign policy? We don't have to have a complicated philosophy other than that we shouldn't initiate wars." Daniel McAdams, the group's executive director who advised Paul on foreign affairs for several years, said, "If we have no more wars, we'll have been successful."[200] The institute will monitor foreign policy legislation, keeping voting scores, and promoting a Libertarian foreign policy perspective through speeches and articles.

As more people become self-educated on matters of politics and of the Liberty movement, this catalyzed group of activists and voters can very well hold the key to future election outcomes, whether it gains influence within the Republican Party over time or whether it remains separate and autonomous. If the movement's numbers grow further, this will bolster its position in becoming a potentially strong, dynamic force in swinging national elections. This would appear especially so if Americans become further disillusioned with the actions of both national parties.

Those in America and abroad who believe that the change that is happening in the world today—including America—is for the worse should become pro-active to help change the course of history. Those ills that require corrective actions include globalization, control by the few over the many, the growing disparity in income/wealth distribution, the increased tendency to go to war rather than use it as a last resort, increased foreign interventionism everywhere in the name of national security or promoting democracy/human rights, the use of unmanned drones which indiscriminately kill civilians including little children,

---

[198] Michael Polito, "Ron Paul launches 'Institute for Peace," National Review, http://www.nationalreview.com/corner/345877, April 17, 2013.

[199] "The neo-conservative era is dead: Ron Paul announces D.C. think-tank," http://rt.com/usa/, April 12, 2013.

[200] Rosie Gray, "Ron Paul launches foreign policy think tank," http://www.buzzfeed.com, April 17, 2013.

the right of a government to indefinitely detain an American citizen on suspicion without evidence and without habeas corpus under the War on Terror, warrantless searches and access by the Government to Internet e-mails, the Central Bank's unending printing of monies without currency backing only to support more debt and government spending.

Based on its latest post-election analysis report issued in March 2013, the national Republican Party has yet to grasp or fully acknowledge that the national issues Paul addresses are the key issues of the present and future.

For those of us who desire a better nation and world governed by common sense, humanitarianism, economic liberty, the right to life and property as well as the rule of law under the Constitution, the real choice in 2012 was presidential candidate Dr. Ron Paul. It appears he will continue to be the real statesman in this twenty-first century. It is apparent that the Congress and the presidency are further drifting away from what the Founding Fathers had envisioned. And that is to the detriment of America and its prior highly esteemed status among the many nations of the world.

# CHAPTER FIVE

# Ron Paul Support Grows Abroad

WHEN MITT ROMNEY was visiting Poland, Fox News host Greta Van Susteren noted Ron Paul supporters in the streets of Poland. She interviewed a Poland national who politely answered when she asked if they came to the square to see Governor Romney:

> We came out here just to say hello. And to tell him [Romney] that we're not interested in his candidacy; we are interested in Ron Paul and what he says, because he is the one that really makes a difference. He's the one that says about our troops coming back to Poland and not dying with American troops out there. And he is the only one that says about the visas problem, because this is something that is very distracting for us, you know. Polish people have to go and ask for the opportunity to go to the U.S.A. to have a trip. And this is awful for us. And, Ron Paul talks about demolishing the system, not changing or altering it in any way. He's just saying about completely destroying it. And this is what we think should be done.[201]

In answer to Van Susteren's question concerning President Obama, the Paul supporter responded, "We are completely against President Obama. President Obama is a socialist—in Poland, he would even be called a Communist."

CBS photos showed thousands in Gdansk, Poland, where Romney was meeting with Poland Prime Minister Donald Tusk. Among the

---

[201] Daniel Halper, "Ron Paul supporters amass—in Poland," The Weekly Standard, http://www.weeklystandard.com/print/blogs/ron-paul-supporters-amass-poland_649135.html, July 30, 2012.

large crowds, Polish Ron Paul supporters held high a very, very large banner reading "Polish Choice—Ron Paul." In fact, as reported in news accounts, "Ron Paul supporters were all over Romney as the candidate visited the country, showing up in town squares with massive pro-Paul banners and chanting Paul's name outside of meetings." It was reported that a group of pro-Paul Poles organized a Facebook group with a Google translation of the slogan "Poles support the best U.S. president."[202] While the Pole Paul supporters were holding up large banners, news accounts indicated that "volunteers from the Romney campaign struggled in vain to use umbrellas to block a large Ron Paul banner from sight."[203] The Paul supporters came from a newly founded party called Kongres Nowej Prawicy, standing for "Congress of the New Right." The political group has Libertarian/Conservative leanings.

There are other international Paul supporters, including those in Germany, South Africa, France, and Serbia.[204] The fact that an American presidential candidate, known as a constitutionalist, and for his strong economic and foreign policy positions, had a cadre of followers from many nations who believed and showed their support in his liberty campaign, is also amazing. How many American presidential candidates have had this kind of following overseas prior to even becoming a nominee or president? Not many, to my recollection! Yet Ron Paul's revolution attracted many supporters in foreign lands also.

In Madrid, Spain, at a rally of citizens held in a public square in March 2012, a video posted has one of the organizers/speakers at the rally saying,

> We are here for liberty and truth. In this moment a true revolution is forming in the American electoral system. Without any media here in Spain, the candidacy of Ron Paul in the Republican primary in the U.S., for better or for worse, should be treated as big news here in Spain like any globalized country . . . . As one of his campaign promises is to end the American empire. End all wars, withdraw all troops and close all military bases spreading over 134 countries worldwide.

---

[202] Jenny Rogers, "Ron Paul haunts Mitt Romney in Poland," The Examiner (Washington), http://washingtonexaminer.com, July 30, 2012.

[203] Geoffrey Malloy, "Ron Paul supporters photobomb Mitt Romney's visit to Poland," The Daily Caller, http://dailycaller.com, July 30, 2012.

[204] Rosie Gray, "Ron Paul revolution follows Romney to Poland," http://www.buzzfeed.com, July 30, 2012.

The speaker further said,

> In these times of economic crises in which we are constantly at the threshold of war followed by another war, the Spanish people need and deserve this thunder of hope. Our message is Ron Paul and it consists of just that hope. The pacifist policy advocated by Ron Paul is an opportunity for all countries in the world. For this reason and because the media's blackout of Ron Paul . . . and in addition they are constantly spreading wrong accusations and slander to discredit his candidacy, we decided to take the job of the journalist. They get paid—we will see you on the streets.[205]

At the end of February 2012, Germany's largest liberal leaning newspaper published a lengthy online article about Ron Paul and his supporters. According to the individual posting this information on the Daily Paul, the newspaper is comparable to the *New York Times* or the British *Guardian*. The German newspaper article reported about the young supporters of Paul from Ohio and the reasons for their support of his candidacy as well as Paul's biography, highlighting his Conservative fiscal leanings as well as his support for the troops mentioning his anti-war stance. It referenced "End the Fed" and the return to the gold standard and even mentioned the campaign's delegate strategy.[206]

In this age of the Internet and social media, Ron Paul's candidacy and his message were catalyzing tweets and Facebook posts by citizens abroad. There were meet-up groups in Holland whose purpose as cited was "to collect and distribute information about Ron Paul as well as to spread his message of small government, sound money, non-interventionist foreign policy and liberty."[207]

Starting back in 2008, during Paul's prior GOP presidential candidacy, foreigners abroad supported his campaign and policies. Again, in 2011-2012, that support continued. The "Ron Paul Sign Bomb" campaign on October 10, 2011, indicated an organization set up for that purpose from countries like France, Spain, Italy, Ireland, Serbia, Australia,

---

[205] "Spain for Ron Paul" (http://youtu.be/zbvVAkoswks), http://www.dailypaul.com/228743, Madrid, Spain, April 25, 2012.

[206] "Germany's highest-circulating national newspaper: 'Why America's youth is enthusiastic about Ron Paul,'" http://www.dailypaul.com, March 4, 2012.

[207] http://wwwmeetup.com/RonPaulHolland/,(accessed February 24, 2013).

Germany, Croatia, South Africa, Switzerland, Netherlands, Estonia, Czech Republic, and Slovakia. The website stated, "We hope you will support the election of Ron Paul and stand united with Americans . . . as our brothers and sisters in Liberty—not just for us, but the entire world! Revolutions are breaking out all over the world and we stand united!!! Ron Paul is the only U.S. presidential candidate of this election to truly understand the philosophy of liberty!" The campaign was calling on people to lead a group in the respective countries to support Paul.[208]

Some posts by individuals underscored the need for greater freedom and the connection to Ron Paul's philosophy as a U.S. presidential candidate. From France, Benoit Malbranque posted on the sign bomb.

> You've described the situation of your country as highly bad. Don't forget that you're still, for most Europeans, the country of freedom. As far as I'm concerned, I hope the U.S. will take the lead for a counter-revolution (like the one Thatcher and Reagan led back in the early 80's). The future of our freedom is mostly in your hands, you Americans.[209]

Michael Pleamoinn wrote on the Ron Paul Sign Bomb in Ireland that "Ron Paul has many supporters in Ireland. The idea of a Sign Bomb is an ideal way to bring all those people together. The message of peace, personal liberty and prosperity is spreading." There was Bradleigh Yaworsky of Australia, posting his comment, saying, "I looked up Ron Paul in the thesaurus. It came back with integrity." Then there was the young woman whose photo was posted on the Ron Paul sign bomb Croatia. She was holding a white placard that read, "Ron Paul 2012; Hope for America, Hope for Croatia, Hope for the world." There was the photo of people in a line on a busy street in the Netherlands, young and middle-aged individuals holding Ron Paul campaign signs, "Ron Paul 2012, Restore America Now." Carl Michael's posted comments on the Netherlands sign bomb saying, "I sincerely hope that our efforts will help to promote the philosophy of Dr. Ron Paul over here."[210]

---

[208] http://www.ronpaulsignbomb.com/other-countries.html (accessed February 24, 2013).

[209] Ibid.

[210] Ibid.

A video of those who joined the Ron Paul sign bomb in Estonia showed a group of people holding large signs, "Google: Ron Paul; Join the Revolution." As noted on the Paul Sign Bomb website, a message was posted having seen the Estonia video from Ron Paul supporters that simply said, "We are so pleased to see the worldwide support Ron Paul is receiving and we stand united with our brothers and sisters across the globe in this fight for liberty!"

There were European Ron Paul meetups, Ron Paul T-shirts bought online, Europe4RonPaul blogspots, and European Ron Paul meetups in Amsterdam, the Netherlands; Antwerpen, Belgium; Athlone, Ireland; Barcelona, Madrid, Spain; Berlin, Bonn, Frankfurt, Hamburg, Karlsruhe, Kaiserslautern, Munich, Germany; Bratislava, Slovakia, Brno, Prague, Czech Republic; Edinburgh, Scotland; Helsinki, Finland; Lisbon, Portugal, London, England; Oslo, Norway; Paris, France; Sion, Zurich, Switzerland; Verona, Italy; Vienna, Austria (http://europe4ronpaul. blogspot.com/). There were worldwide Ron Paul blogs and websites including Asia for Ron Paul, Brazil for Ron Paul, Canadians for Ron Paul, Daily Paul from the USA, Indians and Pakistanis for Ron Paul, Ron Paul Venezuela.[211]

Ron Paul is getting invitations to speak outside this country too. He spoke at the Manning Networking Conference in Ottawa, a major Canadian gathering of Conservative leaders, in Canada on March 8, 2013. Anticipating attending the conference, a Canadian posted on DailyPaul.com that "considering Ron Paul is coming to Ottawa and my wife and I will be going to see him speak . . . we are a little more than excited."[212]

His speech was well received. He outlined major challenges America is confronting, echoing many of the themes he addressed during the course of his presidential campaign and during his tenure in Congress.[213] He discussed issues like president-approved drone assassinations, abortion, deception by the government, and central bankers. Preston Manning

---

[211]  http://europe4ronpaul.blogspot.com/ (accessed February 24, 2013).

[212]  "Ron Paul comes to (goes to) Ottawa!", http://www.DailyPaul.com, March 7, 2013.

[213]  http://en.video.canoe.tv/video/featured/entertainment/2434063121001/ron-paulspirit- of- liberty-lives- in-Canada/2212275015001 (accessed March 8, 2013).

DEBORAH K. SMARTH

entertained a questions and answers session with Dr. Paul and fielded questions from those attending.[214]

As Dr. Paul said often on the campaign trail in 2012, you cannot stop ideas whose time has come. The liberty message of the 2012 Paul presidential candidacy is popular. As more people understand what he stood for and his comprehensive solutions to current economic decline and halting a dangerous empire building foreign policy, the message will catch on further. The message of liberty is universal, and the fact that he had such a loyal following in America and abroad is evidence, indeed. As Dr. Paul said many times, the cause of liberty brings people together. That is a winning coalition for the world.

---

[214] http://www.ronpaul.com/2013/03/08/ron-paul-qa-session-with-preston-manning-at-2013-manning-networking-conference/.

# CHAPTER SIX

# Conclusion

## Lessons Drawn from the 2012
## Presidential Election Outcome

THE AMERICAN ELECTORAL system presents inequities and is clearly not structured in the most optimum way to promote fair elections so that the populace and grassroots control the inevitable presidential nominee of either party or the general election victor. Despite the strong, swelling grassroots support by Paul activists at individual local precinct, district, and state GOP conventions, in the end, the existing apparatus of the powerful party structure crushed such bottom-up efforts. Both national parties, through their party regulars and rank-and-file party committee members who take instructions from the top, control which candidates they want to proceed and which presidential candidate will receive the party coronation for the presidency. The same observation can very well apply to other lesser elective offices.

Even though America has been praised and may be looked at by the vast majority of Americans and by others in foreign countries as having a truly free and open democratic process through its election ballot, it is clear that many factors can impede a truly free election. Clearly, what happened during the 2012 GOP presidential nomination process indicates the system is not as transparent, open, and free as one would imagine. That is why, despite the change of guard in the Office of the Presidency through national elections every four years and the change of guard that occurs in the composition of the U.S. Congress in various election cycles, no real positive systemic changes seem to transpire for the good of all. These conditions are further complicated by the "Fourth Estate" that has proven itself to be a biased media, more than often, not adhering to the highest standards of journalism concerning objectivity and truthfulness.

The third party political action committees and "super PACs," allowed to raise and spend funds on behalf of presidential candidates, pumps enormous sums of monies into the nomination and subsequent general election process. This was clearly the case in the recent 2012 presidential election, which was record-breaking in terms of expenditures reaching more than two billion dollars. The two presidential candidates who faced off in the general election received most of their funds from the seasoned elites and the money class (i.e., the one percenters, bankers, and corporate institutions). According to an Associated Press news account, Obama raised nearly $1 billion to defeat GOP presidential candidate Mitt Romney. There were 770 top donors, who raised up to $268 million for his re-election campaign, and 250 campaign bundlers, who each raised at minimum $500,000 for Obama.[215]

How can the American people compete with the massive amounts of monies that are raised and expended for information campaigns that are slanted, oftentimes untruthful, and disingenuous on behalf of their anointed candidates? How can the American people make informed decisions about how they will vote or how they can influence who will be nominated for the highest office of the land and evidently have their candidate compete in the national election? Despite Paul's army of activists and millions of supporters, they could not deliver his nomination as the balance of power rested with the media and political establishment as well as the elite interests who control party politics and policy decisions.

In 2012, several GOP state primaries and caucuses, many of which were beauty contests only, were alleged to be fraudulent, resulting in the resignations of some state GOP chairs. The selection of delegates to the national convention at local, county, or district and then state conventions was an arduous process controlled for the most part by party insiders who tirelessly tried to prevent—through rules manipulation and other unethical practices—the Paul delegates from walking away with state convention wins. This book documents the numerous uphill battles in which supporters and delegates of Ron Paul were engaged in order to attain victories at these state party conventions. Then, even after all their

---

[215] Ken Thomas, "Obama campaign fundraisers: List of top donors releases," Huffington Post, http://www.huffingtonpost.com, March 2, 2013.

hard work and through their knowledge of Robert's Rules of Order and other party rules in their attainment of convention wins—despite the gamesmanship of party regulars—many Paul delegates in different state delegations were being de-credentialed at the national GOP convention.

In addition, the national party machinery changed the rules at the national convention to essentially rob the Paul campaign and its grassroots delegates of the ability to put Ron Paul's name in nomination. The five-state plurality of delegates rule was changed to eight states at the national convention even though the five-state plurality rule was the one which legitimately governed the 2012 GOP state convention process up to the national convention. To further prevent any possibility of an automatic speech as a result of having Paul's name in nomination, the RNC literally took away credentials from Paul delegates that had already won at prior state conventions. By any standards, the party leadership's practices that were executed were not open or transparent at all. Indeed, this behavior was not welcoming to party newcomers, which included Latinos, African Americans, gays, and youth, etc. In fact, as already alluded to in this book, former national RNC chairman Michael Steele openly criticized what had been done to Dr. Paul and his supporters during the national convention proceedings. And on the March 8, 2013, *Morning Joe* political talk show, Steele again commented about how such treatment just offended new party activists and prevents the party from enlarging its tent.

Any reasonable person looking at all of these developments and circumstances has to conclude that the behavior and actions of the party "power holders and brokers" were not ethical. Any reasonable person looking at the continuum of reporting coverage and news accounts via the corporate national media, often referred to as the mainstream media (MSM), concerning presidential candidate Ron Paul and his campaign supporters, would also have to conclude that the media, with the exception of a notable few (i.e., John Stossel, Neil Cavuto of Fox News, NPR, etc.) were untruthful, biased, and dismissive of this particular candidate. Pew research studies indicated that Paul did receive far less coverage even though he was the last standing candidate against Mitt Romney. Through the early part of 2013, reporters and commentators have yet to acknowledge the influence of Ron Paul's presidential candidacy in establishing a vocal, strong Libertarian wing of the Republican Party. They generally have not acknowledged his influence on the debate and discussions in American politics that are occurring currently, concerning interventionist pre-emptive and undeclared wars, the use of unmanned drones, the use of the military to arrest citizens on U.S. soil "on suspicion only" and without due process, and the potential, indefinite detention of citizens allowed under the NDAA. He was the only GOP presidential candidate speaking about these issues, constitutional principles, and civil liberties in the national presidential debates and during the presidential nomination campaign trail. It is interesting to note that Senator Rand Paul of Kentucky has continued to elevate these issues in the U.S. Senate, following in his father's footsteps. This was the case during his March 2013 Senate filibuster concerning the use of drones to kill citizens on American soil, forcing the Obama administration to respond through U.S. attorney general Eric Holder that no drones could be used to kill citizens on American soil.

The same cavalier, dismissive, and offensive commentaries appear from the usual media pundits, however. Take, for instance, *New York* magazine political writer John Heilemann commenting on Joe Scarborough's March 8, 2013, show, referencing Ron Paul's ideas on certain issues as consisting of "kookiness." He said, "If you take away the kookiness of it, if you just focus on the stuff that's appealing."[216] Kookiness! Really? To whom? Paul's ideas proved to connect with millions of voters. Heilemann also inaccurately described Paul as "an isolationist." Paul is a non-interventionist, not an isolationist. He continually clarified that point over and over again for members of the press throughout his long campaign. During that segment of the Joe Scarborough show, Steve Schmidt, a campaign and public relations strategist for the national Republican Party, also commented that "there's going to be a big, robust debate that plays out over the next couple of years and what has been a strain of libertarianism in the Republican party that's had no expression for a long time is going to begin to express itself . . . . We're going to have a big foreign policy debate in the Republican Party headed into 2016."[217] He was referring to the knee-jerk interventionism of America's current foreign policy. That big debate, after all, emanates from Ron Paul's 2008 and 2012 Republican presidential candidacy in which he promoted a non-interventionist foreign policy, and it proved popular with those who

---

[216] Transcript of the Joe Scarborough show, "Morning Joe," March 8, 2013, Video, http://www.nbcnews.com/id/3036789/ns/msnbc-morning_joe/vp/51097838#51097838.

[217] Ibid.

knew about his position on this issue. If the media would have reported as truthful journalists on Paul's positions in 2012, more people would have rallied around his commonsense approach in solving the ills of this nation and world, attracted by his longtime record of integrity and unflinching resolve and courage to raise issues that may not fit into the establishment's politically correctness model.

Paul's record speaks for itself, and that is why Ron Paul has such a strong following. He has inspired so many people—with more than two million votes cast for him in the primary and caucus states—despite the poor media coverage and the documented lower percentage of press coverage for his candidacy and campaign as a whole when compared to other GOP presidential contenders. He won more than the necessary five states' plurality of delegates to have one's name placed in nomination under RNC Rule 40 adopted at the 2008 national GOP convention, which was supposed to govern the 2012 national convention. But these outcomes were halted by a national party leadership that feared the possibility of a Paul speech on the floor or a brokered convention. So they resorted to changing the rules in Tampa.

The many observations and examples shared with the reader throughout these chapters show how the formal party structure, from top to bottom, was not open to new individuals who wanted to participate and engage in the political process in order to impact on their respective states' delegates being sent to the national convention in Tampa, Florida in August 2012. Quite to the contrary, the occurrences which took place until the very last state convention held in July 2012 in Nebraska were eye-opening inasmuch as the party structure tried to prevent these phenomenal wins by presidential candidate Ron Paul.

On the way to Tampa and at the national GOP convention, the national "Party" apparatus outright de-credentialed Paul delegates to reduce the number of states in which Paul held a plurality of delegates. The Rules Committee, which met prior to the opening of the GOP Nominating Convention, essentially changed the rules on the spot to raise the minimum threshold to eight states from five states' plurality of delegates, adopted at the 2008 presidential convention, allowing a presidential candidate's name to be placed in nomination and entitling that candidate to a fifteen-minute speech on the floor of the convention.

In addition, the RNC also initially proposed rules to prevent any such grassroots participation leading to potential victories at state conventions from ever happening again. Those RNC rule proposals would have rendered state conventions useless by allowing the preferred or presumptive presidential nominee to have veto power over delegates who are typically chosen at local, county, district, and state convention levels. These proposed rule changes on delegates' selection to the national convention triggered such outrage while the committee meetings were being held in Tampa that the RNC dropped them. Yet they did pass revised rules which require that delegate allocation be decided by a statewide presidential primary or caucus, notwithstanding a state's individual rules. In the 2012 election, despite the fact that there were primaries and caucuses, the rules in different states allowed delegates to be chosen at county, district, and state conventions regardless of the outcomes of primary and caucus elections. Finally, the national Republican Party passed a rule to allow the RNC to have the power to change rules for the 2016 convention without input from the party rank and file delegates. Traditionally, rules for the national convention are considered and voted upon by delegates of the prior convention. Following the Tampa Convention, individual state party committees, like New Hampshire, passed resolutions to condemn the rule changes since the rules limit grassroots input within the national party.

Ironically, when the RNC held its spring meeting in April 2013, well-known Conservative Republican Morton Blackwell from Virginia attempted to repeal the rules adopted in Tampa, but as reported by Campaign for Liberty, "party insiders defeated Morton Blackwell's resolution from clearing the Rules Committee and making it to the floor for a full vote."[218]

While the technicalities of party rules can be debated, this book did not examine all the technical aspects of "bound" versus "unbound" delegates. Getting into arcane rules and interpretations of rules would not serve a purpose. However, it is interesting to point out that award winning journalist Ben Swann had indicated after communicating with a member of the RNC Rules Committee that "binding and non-binding distinctions do not have an effect on nominating a candidate's name. If 'binding' is allowable by rule (it is not), it would only pertain to a vote taken on the nomination, not the process of placing a name in nomination."[219]

---

[218] John Tate, letter to supporters, April 14, 2013.

[219] Ben Swann, "Three facts about a candidate's name being placed into nomination at the Republican National Convention," http://www.dailypaul.com/244870/, July 16, 2012.

The intent of this book focuses solely on letting the average American voter understand how they were not being informed by the media about what was happening at state GOP conventions across the country prior to the national convention or were they thoroughly informed about the anomalies in vote tallies in the early primary and caucus states. Poor media coverage only served to further assist the national Republican Party in providing for the coronation of presidential candidate Mitt Romney. In fact, the American public did not receive appropriate levels of coverage about presidential candidate Ron Paul, and the media's treatment of his candidacy led many to believe that he was unelectable. Oftentimes, the media promoted an image that Paul was a "fringe" candidate. By setting their own issues agenda for campaign coverage and casting attitudes about Paul's candidacy, the media inevitably impacted on the perception by American voters of Paul's candidacy and his prospects in winning the nomination. Many voters did not even realize Paul was in the race until the very end. The media's tendency in covering Paul's candidacy always appeared to be "editorial commentator" and "opinion maker" rather than reporting the facts as they existed.

The treatment that Paul delegates received at the national convention said it all. They were not welcome with open arms as the RNC was committed to and strongly bent on a Mitt Romney nomination. Ron Paul delegates and supporters' signs were confiscated. Yet the convention hall in Tampa had clearly been marked by Paul supporters' presence. As one Paul supporter described the scene, "One literally could not walk 20 feet in the convention center without spotting a Ron Paul button—on delegates, guests, even media. Strangers would break into grins and bear hug one another to the astonishment of wide-eyed neoconservatives, taken aback at how every other young person in attendance seemed to be a supporter of a 77-year old obstetrician from Lake Jackson, Texas."[220] To the dismay of many, Ron Paul supporters and delegates, the Republican leadership presiding over the convention wouldn't even allow the number of votes Paul received in individual state delegations be announced from the podium, even though he had substantial support and the majority of delegates in several states.

The actions of political operatives, like attorney Ben Ginsberg and former governor John Sununu and other Romney campaign advisors

---

[220] Hamdan Azhar, "Love and Politics: Why I'm voting for Ron Paul," PolicyMic, http://www.policymic.com/articles/18181, November 4, 2012.

and aides, were bent on taking away any remote possibility that the 2012 Tampa Convention could be a "brokered" one. They knew that with their rule changes and delegate de-credentialing tactics, this idea of a brokered convention would be avoided. In fact, it would prevent Paul's name from being put in nomination and prevent the American public from hearing a speech Paul would have been entitled to make on the floor of the convention.

At this juncture in American politics, grassroots actions are needed more than ever. The accountability of our so-called elected officials has dramatically declined. The press, more or less, gives our elected officials cover continually! The only way the American public can ever expect true changes in national policy and politics depends on how well the American voters can educate themselves about each candidate beyond the MSM sound bites, editorial comments, and media pundits' opinions. Had the American people known more about presidential candidate Ron Paul, they would have avoided falling prey to the manipulation of information by the media which frequently did not tell the whole story or the truth. In addition, that would have prevented the parroting of falsities by voters concerning Paul's positions and his candidacy's chances of succeeding as GOP presidential nominee. Thank goodness that there were some reporters at state newspapers, in the national media, and independent media outlets who provided at least some coverage of Ron Paul and the conditions that transpired along the way to Tampa and at the national convention. However, what happened along the way to Tampa and in Tampa was a national story that was never truly broadcast in the manner it deserved to be covered. It should have been elevated to a major story since it involved issues of transparency, ethics, fairness, and deceptive practices that were occurring.

The rule changes concerning the number of states' delegate plurality needed to have one's name put in nomination, in combination with the de-credentialing of Paul delegates, assured that the states that the Paul forces had won could not be counted toward that plurality. Those developments afforded the national Republican Party with the sole opportunity to be in total control, preventing any surprises on the floor of the convention by putting Ron Paul's name in nomination and allowing him thereby to make a speech in prime time.

Preventing the Paul forces and other party regulars, who may have been won over at the convention with a Paul speech to possibly affect the total delegate vote tally on the first round of nomination voting, had to be avoided at all cost. Indeed, this objective was achieved but proved detrimental to a GOP victory on November 6, 2012. A national audience of thirty-five-million-plus never had a chance to listen to a Paul speech at the national Republican convention!

Those Republican Party leaders presiding over the national convention, in fact, denied Paul's vote numbers in each of the state delegations from being announced from the convention podium even though individual state delegation chairs were publicly citing the votes for candidates Romney and Paul when their respective state delegations were called upon. Internet videos show such occurrences for state delegations like Georgia, Maine, Minnesota, Nevada, etc.

While there has been no official study (as of this writing) concerning the effects of Paul supporters in the November 6 election, it is safe to assume that had the national Republican Party chose not to go down the route they did at the national convention, the outcome of the national election may have been quite different. Ron Paul supporters either did not vote or wrote-in Ron Paul's name. The numbers of those sitting out the election and those who wrote-in Ron Paul's name, regardless if their states officially counted the votes or not—combined with the third-party totals received by candidates like Libertarian candidate Gary Johnson and others—could have ultimately tipped the popular and electoral vote victory to Obama over Romney.

Looking back, the national Republican Party should have opened the tent to the Ron Paul delegates and supporters to avoid a situation that fomented as a result of their unethical and disingenuous strategies and tactics to undermine Paul and his army of supporters. They should have openly embraced the opportunity to unite the GOP prior to the national presidential election, welcoming the Liberty wing activists.

Americans may never have such an opportunity again to have a presidential candidate who shone bright as a real statesman, not fearful of taking on the most powerful interests and the establishment's status quo.

But what if more people knew about Ron Paul during the 2012 GOP primaries and caucuses, his policy positions, and his unrelenting integrity throughout his long public career? What if he received greater news media coverage, fairer and more truthful in nature? What if he received bumps in popularity due to appropriate and fair news coverage? What if the rule changes at the national GOP convention never occurred, thereby allowing Ron Paul's name to go in nomination, allowing Paul to make his fifteen-minute speech on the floor of the convention? What if these events led to a brokered convention and, inevitably, a Ron Paul nomination? Would he have beaten Obama? One observation can be made for sure and that is Paul would have articulately illustrated that there were real sharp differences between him and incumbent president and Democratic Party nominee Barack Obama. The fact is that Paul drew voters from diverse ideological bases—traditional Republican Conservatives who supported shrinking the size and role of Government and reducing government taxation and spending; progressive Democrats, disenchanted with the Obama administration, who supported civil liberties and opposed war; and Independents, who supported a candidate who was not fearful of taking on the political system and the status quo. There is no doubt that a Paul presidency could have begun, curing the many ills that currently exist within our nation and its public policies, both domestic and foreign.

An opportunity in America was missed in 2012 to realize new, positive changes in the Office of the Presidency. Americans witnessed stolen victories in 2012; victories that were stolen from Dr. Paul at State GOP conventions; Paul delegates who were denied their seats at the national convention, quelling the grassroots support that had grown for the Republican "Liberty" candidate, Ron Paul; and due to the party leadership's on-the-spot rule changes, preventing his name from being put in nomination. In a sense, these stolen victories prevented the American people from having a real opportunity to change the course of history. A Paul presidency would have represented a real change in direction for national domestic and economic policies as well as foreign policy. Instead, there was no change of guard in the Office of the Presidency, and there would have been little change, had Romney succeeded in winning over Obama, because both candidates were beholden to the status quo. In fact, both candidates had received large sums of campaign contributions from the Wall Street institutions and banking interests. The only presidential candidate who challenged the status quo and current systems and policies was Ron Paul.

What took place with Ron Paul's seeking the presidential nomination demonstrates that the American people have very little or no control over the election process. Despite his strong populist and grassroots support and victories at many Republican state conventions, in the end, these victories were stolen.

But it is up to all of us now to ensure we regain and control the direction of our Government and nation through strong vigilance at all governmental levels. We must cast our votes for those candidates running for office on the basis of principles and not who the media or establishment deems as their favorite and ordains as the potential winner. We must cast our votes for substance over style. Voters must not mimic or parrot the pronouncements of the media or political establishment, for it becomes accepted as truth when, in fact, it has been proven to be far from the truth.

Wanting the country to return to the vision and principles of the Founding Fathers in support of the U.S. Constitution can be a reality if people learn to go the extra length, obtaining their news from other sources besides the MSM and political establishment. But more importantly, people need to take positions based on their own self-education and research, broadcast their positions, clamoring and making it clear that they will no longer stand for or vote for those individuals who are not committed to rational policies to combat the current state of affairs in our country or those who do not abide by constitutional principles. Why should we support more wars? Why should we agree to more bailouts or the printing of more monies by the Federal Reserve which further encourages congressional/governmental spending and devalues the dollar? Why should we agree to more annual deficits and an increase in the national debt? Why should our elected leaders in Congress put any ally's interests over America's national security and national interests? Why should Americans experience blowback and be put in harm's way as a result of its interventionist foreign and military policies overseas?

America can be restored if all of us—*as citizens*—join together, demanding it be restored to free markets, less aggression, and foreign interventionism. We can demand that the Fed stop printing monies to mask the current economic decline. We can stop the deficits and national debt by shrinking the size of government and understanding its true role in protecting individuals' life, liberty, property, and the pursuit of happiness. We can halt the absurd levels of taxation which prevents people from saving, spending, and enjoying the fruits of their own labor.

We, as Americans, can look to support candidates that are not beholden to any party over the people's interests. Politics is not about how to win at the expense of the American people. Politics should be about how we can shape policies to reflect the people's will, maximizing their freedom and liberty. The first such presidential candidate in this century and the last, who came closest to committing to such high ideals, was Ron Paul. While the leadership and integrity of Ron Paul will continue,

Americans lost a great opportunity to change guard in the Office of the Presidency at a time when it is needed most. The 2012 presidential election was stolen from the American people by a media and political establishment, which were not truthful. The vested interests of the so-called establishment were revealed through the countless executed tactics and strategies aimed at diminishing Paul's victories. The American people must work to prevent such an election outcome from ever happening again. This lost opportunity and stolen victories must serve as an important lesson to the American electorate.

Americans often complain about politicians and empty promises, but in this instance, one candidate stood apart from all the others in terms of actions and deeds as well as honesty and integrity. The people failed to take advantage of this potential opportunity due to misinformation and the false messaging of the political and media establishment and their overreliance on the establishment's reporting instead of seeking answers and knowledge on their own about presidential candidate Paul.

The Paul presidential candidacy and Campaign for Liberty movement has set a new path for Americans to consider and follow. The influence of such activists cannot be underestimated. It is now part of history despite the political and media establishment whispers. We, as Americans, should use that history to prevent such mistakes from ever happening again. America is supposed to have a government for and by the people! Americans can still restore the republic, but it will take continued vigilance, strong commitment, passion, and action as the Paul movement has catalyzed. Americans should join this vigilant revolution of ideas and actions before it is too late.

# THE FOUNDING PRINCIPLES OF GOVERNMENT AS STATED IN THE DECLARATION OF INDEPENDENCE

WE HOLD THESE truths to be self-evident, that all men are created equal, that they are endowed by their Creator with certain unalienable Rights, that among these are Life, Liberty and the pursuit of Happiness. That to secure these rights, Governments are instituted among Men, deriving their just powers from the consent of the governed. That whenever any Form of Government becomes destructive of these ends, it is the Right of the People to alter or to abolish it, and to institute new Government, laying its foundation on such principles, and organizing its powers in such form, as to them shall seem most likely to effect their Safety and Happiness.

# QUOTATIONS THAT MATTER

## *On a Central Bank:*

"As to the assumed authority of any assembly in making paper money, or paper of any kind, a legal tender, or in other language, a compulsive payment, it is a most presumptuous attempt at arbitrary power. There can be no such power in a republican government: the people have no freedom—and property no security—where this practice can be acted."

*—Thomas Paine*

"The central bank is an institution of the most deadly hostility existing against the principles and form of our Constitution. I am an enemy to all banks discounting bills or notes for anything but coin. If the American People allow private banks to control the issuance of their currency, first by inflation and then by deflation, the banks and corporations that will grow up around them will deprive the people of all their property until their children will wake up homeless on the continent their Fathers conquered."

*—Thomas Jefferson*

"We need to take away the government's money power. The banking industry needs its welfare check ended. The dollar's soundness depends on its being untied from the machine that can make an infinite number of copies of dollars and reduce their value to zero.

*—Dr. Ron Paul*

"The Federal Reserve System must be challenged. Ultimately, it needs to be eliminated. The government cannot and should not be trusted with a monopoly on money. In fact, I believe that freedom itself is at stake in this struggle."

*—Dr. Ron Paul*

"The U.S. government has a technology, called a printing press (or, today, its electronic equivalent), that allows it to produce as many U.S. dollars as it wishes at essentially no cost. By increasing the number of U.S. dollars in circulation, or even by credibly threatening to do so, the US government can also reduce the value of a dollar in terms of goods and services, which is equivalent to raising the prices in dollars of those goods and services. We conclude that, under a paper-money system, a determined government can always generate higher spending and hence positive inflation."

—*Ben Bernanke*, *Federal Reserve chairman*

## *On Freedom, Liberty, and Religion:*

"Only a virtuous people are capable of freedom. As nations become more corrupt and vicious they have more need of masters."

—*Benjamin Franklin*

"Convinced that the people are the only safe depositories of their own liberty, and that they are not safe unless enlightened to a certain degree, I have looked on our present state of liberty as a short-lived possession unless the mass of the people could be informed to a certain degree."

—*Thomas Jefferson*

"I know no safe depository of the ultimate powers of the society but the people themselves; and if we think them not enlightened enough to exercise their control with a wholesome discretion, the remedy is not to take it from them, but to inform their discretion by education. This is the true corrective of abuses of constitutional power."

—*Thomas Jefferson*

"The people are the ultimate guardians of their own liberty."

—*Thomas Jefferson*

"Certainly the drafters of the Declaration of Independence and the Constitution, both replete with references to God, would be aghast at the federal government's hostility to religion. The establishment clause of the First Amendment was simply intended to forbid the creation of an official state church like the Church of England, not to drive religion out of public life.

—*Dr. Ron Paul*

"Any effort to mandate or enforce the goal of making everyone free from want and fear through government action will guarantee the destruction of the concept of personal liberty. Whether it's local government or world government, and no matter the motivation, this effort can only destroy one's right to life, liberty, and property."

—*Dr. Ron Paul*

## On Peace and a Republican Form of Government:

"The true foundation of republican government is the equal right of every citizen in his person and property and in their management."

—*Thomas Jefferson*

"The spirit of monarchy is war and enlargement of domain; peace and moderation are the spirit of a republic."

—*Thomas Jefferson*

"Peace and friendship with all mankind is our wisest policy, and I wish we may be permitted to pursue it."

—*Thomas Jefferson*

"Unlike those nations whose rulers use their country's resources to seek conquests, to carry on warring contests with one another, and consequently plunge their people into debt and devastation, free societies are organized for the happiness and prosperity of their people, and this is best pursued in a state of peace."

—*Thomas Jefferson*

"War is the health of the state; peace is the health of the people."

—*Dr. Ron Paul*

## Convictions and Principles:

"In matters of style, swim with the current; in matters of principle, stand like a rock."

—*Thomas Jefferson*

"Always vote for principle, though you may vote alone, and you may cherish the sweetest reflection that your vote is never lost."

*—John Quincy Adams*

"Truth is treason in the Empire of Lies."

*—Dr. Ron Paul*

## *Role of Government/Government Actions and Policies:*

"Foreign aid is taking money from the poor people of a rich country and giving it to the rich people of a poor country."

*—Dr. Ron Paul*

"Peace is better than war. Free markets are better than socialism. Balanced budgets are better than spending."

*—Dr. Ron Paul*

"Once you endorse the principle of welfarism, guess what? The poor get poorer, and the rich get richer. It's a totally failed system. And we can't be intimidated by those that argue, 'If you don't support the welfare system, you're not a humanitarian.'"

*—Dr. Ron Paul*

"Government is too big. The role of government ought to be for the protection of liberty, not for the intrusion in economic affairs. We've spent too much, we taxed too much, we borrowed too much. It's bankrupting this country. I've been talking about these problems for a long, long time. Now we're bankrupt and we have to decide which way we're going to go."

*—Dr. Ron Paul*

"The prevailing attitude of the American people is that everyone has a right to medical care. This is an intellectual error that will lead us down a path toward destroying what is good in the current system."

*—Dr. Ron Paul*

"People often say that what this country needs is for people in Washington to stop fighting and just get the job done. To achieve that, we need more 'bipartisanship.' I don't agree . . . When the ideas of both parties are bad, there is really only one hope: That they will continue fighting and not pass any new legislation."

—*Dr. Ron Paul*

## *Government Drones and Assassinations:*

"When the president kills without due process, he disobeys the laws he has sworn to uphold, no matter who agrees with him. When we talk about killing as if it were golf, we debase ourselves. And when the government kills and we put our heads in the sand, woe to us when there is no place to hide."

—*Judge Andrew Napolitano*

"This dramatic increase in the use of drones and the lowered threshold for their use to kill foreigners has tremendous implications for our national security. At home, some claim the use of drones reduces risk to American service members. But this can be true only in the most shortsighted sense. Internationally, the expanded use of drones is wildly unpopular and in fact creates more enemies than it eliminates."

—*Dr. Ron Paul*

# INDEX

## A

ABC, 76
activists, 101, 105, 108, 114, 123, 133
affidavit, 40-41
Afghanistan, 9, 76, 106
agreement, 59, 63, 106, 110
Aitken, Jane, 94
Alaska, 27, 57, 65, 108
Alley, Allen, 36-37
America, 9, 12, 18, 21, 47, 55, 91, 106,
    108, 113-14, 119, 121-22, 131-32
American citizens, 18, 49, 115
American presidential candidates, 117
anomalies, 20, 23, 87, 128
Armstrong, Tom, 36
Associated Press, 33, 42, 44, 51, 63,
    88, 100, 123
Azhar, Hamdan, 30-31, 93, 98, 128

## B

Bachmann, Michele (congresswoman),
    14, 18, 75, 77-78
ballot, 26, 39, 43, 52, 61, 93
    first, 28, 52, 57, 84, 92
Barbour, Haley (former governor), 66,
    103
Bauer, Gary, 103
Benton, Jesse, 29, 37, 55, 75
biases, 80, 85, 87

Bin Laden, Osama, 11, 55, 81, 106
Bishop, Greg, 42
Blackwell, Morton, 59, 64, 67, 103
Blitzer, Wolf, 68
blogs, 16, 30, 33-34, 38, 41, 43, 69,
    73, 76, 83
*Boston Globe*, the, 13, 40-41
Brown, Debbie, 107
Bunce, Carl, 64
Bush, George W., 8, 27, 56, 112
*Business Insider*, 29, 84-85

## C

Cain, Herman, 18, 77-78, 88
Campaign for Liberty, 102, 104, 127
    movement of, 133
campaign trail, 76, 91, 95, 99, 112,
    121
candidacy, 10, 12, 15, 55-56, 73,
    75-76, 78, 84, 87, 96, 110,
    116-18, 124, 126, 128
caucus states, 23, 46, 52, 87, 126, 128
Cavuto, Neil, 94, 124
Christie, Chris (governor), 98
citizens, 7, 16-19, 43, 50, 89, 117-18,
    125, 132, 137
Claros, Carol, 41
CNN, 24, 60, 69, 74, 81
Cobb County, 108
college campuses, 11, 45, 101, 105

Colorado, 13, 27, 29, 37-38, 44, 62, 66, 99

Commission on Presidential Debates, 110

committee, 27, 44, 49-51, 62, 99-100, 107

Congress, 7-8, 10, 12, 16, 45, 95, 99, 104, 112-13, 115, 120, 122, 132

Constitution, 7-8, 10, 18, 21, 29, 62, 92, 115, 132, 135-36

Convention Rules Committee, 103

corporate media, 7, 16, 45-46, 50, 86, 111

counties, 13, 24-25, 27-29, 38, 46, 87, 123, 127

Croatia, 119

Czech Republic, 119-20

## D

*Daily Paul*, the, 55, 87, 118, 120

Daughtry, Bryan, 69

Davis, Charles, 60

debt, 8-10, 91, 115, 137

deficits, 10, 80, 109, 132

DeGroot, Ani, 100

delegates
  elected, 31, 34, 41, 53, 58, 62
  grassroots, 14, 124
  plurality of, 14, 21, 64, 83, 126, 129

delegate strategy, 26

delegations, 33, 36-37, 45, 59, 66, 68, 90, 97, 104

democracy, 23, 58, 84, 91

democratic process, 36, 89

district, 23, 28, 31, 35, 87, 122-23, 127

Doherty, Brian, 111

Doherty, Michael (state senator), 11

drones, 17-18, 114, 125, 139

Duncan, John (congressman), 113

## E

Ebke, Laura, 38

election, 14, 24, 43, 72, 86, 97-98, 102, 108, 110, 119, 127, 130
  general, 20, 91, 97-98, 108, 123
  national, 114, 122-23, 130

Erickson, Kevin (pastor), 50

Estonia, 119-20

*Examiner*, the, 23, 83

## F

Fallin, Mary (governor), 34

FEC (Federal Election Commission), 18

Federal Reserve, 10, 15, 49-50, 57, 85-86, 90-91, 95-96, 132, 136

Florida, 44-45, 48-49, 98-99, 126

foreign policy, 8, 15, 17, 26, 55, 74, 76, 91-92, 97-98, 106, 114, 118, 121, 125, 131

Founding Fathers, 8, 16, 21, 73, 87, 115, 132

Fox News, 43, 45, 47, 75, 80, 92-93, 96, 98, 116, 124

France, 117-20

Fredricks, Melinda, 66

freedom, 19, 113, 119, 132, 135-36

## G

Gee, Kathleen, 65

Germany, 10, 117-20

Gingrich, Newt, 14, 18, 24-26, 77-79, 82, 88

Ginsberg, Ben, 34, 67, 103

Glaser, John, 9

Goodman, Amy, 58, 84

GOP, 12-14, 28, 32, 47-48, 52, 93, 96, 98-100, 102, 109, 130 establishment, 33, 43, 46, 52, 55, 62, 66, 108

nomination, 20, 65, 73-74

presidential candidates, 14, 16, 25, 66, 102, 125

presidential nomination process, 20, 122

state conventions, 13, 33, 98, 109

government, 5, 7, 16-17, 19, 24, 45, 54, 56, 87, 97, 105, 112, 115, 118, 131-39

grassroots campaign, 27, 96

### H

Hannity, Sean, 93-94

Hedges, Christopher, 18

Helwig, Alex, 30

Herford, Henry, Jr., 30

Hunter, Jack, 55

### I

integrity, 109, 119, 126, 132-33

Internet, 7-8, 10-11, 16, 35, 46, 54-55, 73, 84, 112, 118

Iowa, 23-24, 27-29, 31, 44, 47, 57, 59, 65, 73, 82-83, 100

Iran, 85, 105-6

Iraq, 9, 94

Iraq War, 9

Ireland, 118-20

Ivutin, Oleg, 108

### J

Jefferson, Thomas, 8, 135-37

Johnson, Bernie, 50

Johnson, Gary (former governor), 92, 95-97, 110, 130

Jones, Walter (congressman), 113

journalism, 73-74, 77-78

journalists, 18, 72-73, 77, 118

### K

Kenney, Evan, 41

Kentucky, 45, 53, 55, 99, 125

Kibbe, Matt, 104

Klobuchar, Amy (senator), 44

Koerner, Robin, 69

Kucinich, Dennis (former congressman), 113-14

### L

Larson, Mat, 94

League of Women Voters, 110

Leno, Jay, 91

LePage, Paul (governor), 15

libertarianism, 111, 125

Linzy, Brad, 58

List, Robert, 58

Louisiana, 13, 27, 29-31, 44, 60-61, 63, 66, 99

### M

Madrid, 117-18, 120

Maine, 13, 15, 25, 27, 29, 33-34, 43-44, 49, 51, 57, 65, 67, 83, 99, 130

Maine Caucus, 24

mainstream media, 7, 11, 19-20, 73-74, 83-87, 124

Massachusetts, 7, 13, 27, 41, 61, 63

Massie, Thomas (congressman), 99, 113

McAdams, Daniel, 114

McDonald, Matthew, 61

McDonnell, Bob (governor), 49

media, 10-12, 17, 20, 23-27, 48, 52,

72-79, 81-89, 110-11, 117,
    123-24, 126, 128-29, 132-33
blackout, 43, 72, 81, 84
coverage, 11, 75, 77, 79, 82, 87,
    126, 128
Mendros, Stavros, 51, 61
Michigan, 27, 45, 99
military, 9, 14, 17-18, 77, 82, 94,
    105, 125
Millette, Russ, 107
Minnesota, 14, 27-28, 31, 44, 49-50,
    57, 59, 65, 82-83, 90, 99, 130
Missouri, 13, 27-29, 43-44, 99
Morgan, Piers, 29
Morrise, Judy, 37
MSNBC, 38, 83, 86
Mulshine, Paul, 106
Murkowski, Lisa (senator), 27

**N**

Napolitano, Andrew, 18, 96, 113
national convention, 13-15, 21,
    29-33, 37, 39-40, 47-48, 51-53,
    56-57, 60-64, 71, 92-93, 96-99,
    108-9, 123-24, 126-31
national debt, 8, 10, 18, 80, 86, 132
national GOP convention, 18, 39, 77,
    88, 90, 92, 103, 111, 124, 126,
    130
national parties, 12, 15, 97, 107, 110,
    114, 122, 127
National Republican Party, 15, 28,
    115, 125, 127-30
*National Review*, 67
national security, 114, 132, 139
nations, 8, 10-11, 16-17, 19, 27, 33,
    55, 106, 115, 117, 126, 131,
    136-37
NDAA (National Defense Authorization
    Act), 18, 49-50, 125

Nebraska, 39, 83, 126
Nejedly, Charlie, 34, 41
Nevada, 13-14, 24, 27, 29, 32-33,
    43-44, 58, 61, 64-66, 130
New Hampshire, 73, 82, 93, 98
*New York Times*, the, 18, 53, 57, 65,
    87, 96, 118
nomination process, 21, 33, 37, 58,
    84, 88, 99, 104

**O**

Obama, Barack, 17, 71, 91, 94-95, 97
Obama administration, 8, 17, 76, 96,
    125, 131
Oregon, 13, 36, 57, 65
Ottawa, 120

**P**

Palin, Sarah (former governor), 66,
    77-78, 108
Pappas, Max, 93
party insiders, 13, 103-4, 123, 127
party leaders, 13, 36, 45, 67-68, 99,
    109, 112, 126
Paul, Rand (senator), 53, 55, 68, 125
Paul, Ron, 10-17, 19-20, 23-29,
    36-37, 42-44, 46-50, 52-59, 63,
    73-87, 91-97, 99-101, 104-6,
    110-15, 124-26, 130-31
campaign of, 15, 18, 25-26, 34, 39,
    42-43, 49-50, 54, 60, 64, 70, 79,
    82, 99, 111
delegates of, 15, 29, 33-34, 38, 42,
    48-52, 56, 58, 60-61, 64, 66-67,
    70, 87-88, 123-24, 128-29
supporters of, 25, 27-34, 36-37,
    40-41, 44, 46-48, 50-51, 57-59,
    65, 75, 82-83, 85, 94, 97-98, 107
Paul Festival, 57

DEBORAH K. SMARTH

PEJ (Project for Excellence in
    Journalism), 77-78
Perry, Rick (governor), 78, 88, 112
petitions, 19, 42, 58, 65
Pew Study, 77
Philips, Eric, 45
platform, 10, 15, 20-21, 50, 70, 77,
    98, 105
Poland, 116
policies, 12, 16, 19, 50, 82, 86, 110,
    112, 118, 131-32, 138
political establishment, 12, 15-16, 20,
    44, 123, 132-33
*Politico*, 41, 76
polls, 43, 73, 78-79, 94, 96, 99, 109
Post-Tampa Convention, 5, 90
precincts, 13, 23-25, 28
presidency, 8, 10, 20, 85, 115, 122,
    131, 133
presidential campaign, 7, 10, 12, 19, 47,
    73, 78-79, 85, 89, 97, 99, 104, 120
presidential candidate, 7, 14-16,
    18-21, 33, 43, 48, 77-78, 86, 99,
    105, 109-11, 115, 119, 122-23,
    130-32
presidential election, 7, 92, 96, 98,
    101, 108, 123, 133
presidential race, 18, 43, 79, 82
Priebus, Reince, 33, 68, 99-100, 102-4

R

*Reason*, 75, 111
Renfrow, Kevin, 36
Republican candidates, 7, 75, 78, 99,
    106
Republican National Convention, 34,
    41, 43-44, 47, 54, 56-59, 61-63,
    82, 84, 98, 107
Republican nomination, 7, 12, 43,
    77-78, 80, 85, 96

Republican Party, 8, 15, 23, 28, 30,
    39, 42-45, 56-57, 97, 100-101,
    105-6, 110, 114, 124-25, 130
Republicans, 12, 15, 33-34, 38, 44,
    47-48, 53, 56, 58, 63-64, 70-71,
    79, 92, 104-5, 108
Republican state conventions, 13, 26,
    43, 45, 50, 73, 131
RNC (Republican National
    Committee), 14-15, 28, 32, 37,
    39-40, 44, 48, 51, 53-54, 57-65,
    68-69, 71, 84, 99-104, 126-28
Roberts, John, 80
Robert's Rules of Order, 13, 35-36,
    124
Rockwell, Lew, 69, 113
Romney, Mitt, 13-16, 20-21, 23-35,
    37-41, 43, 45, 51-58, 61-63,
    66-67, 70-71, 73-75, 77-79,
    91-97, 106-7, 116-17
Romney campaign, 15, 34-35, 49,
    52-53, 55, 65, 70, 103, 117
Romney delegates, 37, 61, 66, 93
Ron Paul Revolution PAC, 86
Ron Paul Sign Bomb campaign, 118
Rove, Karl, 98
Ruedrich, Randy, 43
rule changes, 19-20, 50, 59-60, 66-67,
    88, 90, 92-93, 103, 127, 129-30
Rules Committee, 14, 30, 54, 59, 63,
    66, 103-4, 126-27
Ryan, Ashley, 51, 55
Ryan, Paul (congressman), 94-95

S

Santorum, Rick, 18, 23, 25-26, 31,
    37-38, 48, 77, 79, 88
Scarborough, Joe, 85, 125
Scheuer, Michael, 10, 86, 106, 113
Schier, Steven, 113

Schlafly, Phyllis, 103
Schmidt, Steve, 125
Shaikh, Nermeen, 58, 84
Simon, Roger, 75
Slovakia, 119-20
Spain, 117-18, 120
Stafford, Brent, 29
state conventions, 13, 20-21, 23,
    27-35, 38, 40, 42-43, 46, 49, 51,
    60, 66, 74, 123, 126-27
state delegations, 56, 58, 66, 68, 124,
    128, 130
state parties, 28-29, 31, 33, 36, 38,
    41, 93
states, 13-14, 20-21, 24-30, 32-34,
    36, 38, 41-44, 51-52, 58-61,
    63-66, 68, 83, 98-99, 126-30,
    136-37
Stearns, Christopher, 59
Stebbins, Marianne, 44, 49
Steele, Michael, 68-69, 124
Stewart, Jon, 74, 81
Stossel, John, 45, 124
Swann, Ben, 40, 84, 92

### T

Taft, Robert, 70
Tampa, 11, 13-15, 18-19, 21, 28, 39-40,
    47-49, 51-53, 57-58, 74, 88-93,
    98-99, 102-4, 108-9, 126-29
Tarkanian, Amy, 24
Tate, John, 25, 30, 61, 102
Taylor, Jeff, 70
Terhune, Wayne, 65
Texas, 7, 10, 14, 16, 45, 48, 57, 99,
    112, 128
Thorsen, Jesse, 76-77
Tillet, Josiah, 59
Trotta, Liz, 75
Tweed, Brent, 61

### U

United Nations, 9, 16
United States, 8, 18, 20, 49, 74, 84,
    87

### V

Van Susteren, Greta, 116
veterans, 7, 17, 69, 76
Virginia, 27, 29, 59, 64, 66, 98, 112,
    127
voters, 15, 21, 26, 35, 39, 42-43, 69,
    79, 84, 86, 96, 98, 100, 128-29,
    131-32

### W

Washington, 8, 27, 29, 31-32, 38, 40,
    48, 50, 67-68, 82, 112, 117, 139
Washington County, 25, 37
*Washington Times*, the, 60
Wead, Doug, 27-30, 34, 38, 41, 43,
    71, 88-89
Webster, Charlie, 25
White House, 17, 26, 76-77
Williams, Juan, 47
Willis, Mark, 99-100

### Y

YAL (Young Americans for Liberty),
    101